Copyright: Pierre Petiot
ISBN : 978-1-7948-4297-7
Autumn 2021

La Belle Inutile Editions

Printed by www.lulu.com

Ordinary Possessions

Possessions Ordinaires

Contents - Contenu

Photo by Zazie

Ordinary Possessions

Table of Contents

Introduction

In order to suggest the extent of the domain that the following pages attempt to mark out, it is perhaps useful to state how these considerations historically appeared to me, now almost forty years ago, in the years 1980-1985 ...

I remember very well to have then written to a friend: *"Ideas possess us, in an almost voodoo sense of the word."* The point was not then for me to designate a field of an instrumental or technical nature as I will do in the following pages. It was a much more general remark and moreover, initially essentially relating to more properly intellectual domains ...

At the same time, Richard Dawkins published his theory of memes. [Cf. Dawkins, Richard (1989), "11. Memes: the new replicators", *The Selfish Gene* (2nd ed., new ed.), Oxford: Oxford University Press, p. 368, ISBN 0-19-217773-7], although both the idea and the term "memes" have an older origin in his thought.

One of my concerns at the time was to find a plausible meaning to the rather vague concept of *Grands Transparents* as evoked by André Breton. And it seemed to me that ideas and systems of ideas, which, like invisible and abstract viruses 'parasitize' human brains and through them spread across large human groups and even entire civilizations - this without any regard for the interests or even survival of the species - could provide a good example of Grands Transparents.

The idea is quite similar to that of Richard Dawkins' memes. But at the same time it is different, as the basic image behind my point of view is not biological in nature, but rather, let's say , for lack of better wording, "supra biological", or rather maybe "emerging" in relation to biology, in the sense that culture emerges from nature. But it is also of a more general scope than the idea of memes, since it takes into account the fact that we absolutely *cannot* think - nor even humanly exist - without images, ideas or tools. That we should, of course, be wary about images and ideas, because they are not "us" and live an independent life, the current ecological crisis demonstrates it sufficiently, as it originates in philosophical and religious conceptions rooted in the practices inaugurated in the Neolithic period on the one hand, and on the other hand, in the heirs of these long past neolithic practices in the specific case of the capitalist system of thoughts and practices.

But we must necessarily live with images and ideas because in a way they are "us" too. It seems to me that Richard Dawkins's vision is closer to that of viruses parasitizing mankind, while the one I propose is closer to an idea of mandatory *symbiosis*. A symbiosis without which neither images, nor ideas, nor models, nor above all, the human species itself can survive.

As for the Grands Transparents, I learned since then, and in fact quite recently, in *Morphological Interviews, Notebook N ° 1 1936-1944*, a book complied by Germana Ferrari and published by

Editions Sistan Limited in 1987 , that the Grands Transparents idea had been invented by Matta before being taken over by Breton. Matta notes in this regard that Breton gave to his own idea a content quite different from what he himself had in mind when he proposed it to Breton. This was the time when Breton was thinking of a Third Manifesto of Surrealism, and what was aimed at, says Matta, was nothing less than a shift from literary surrealism to a conceptual surrealism. Matta notes that Breton limited the Grands Transparents by making them "anthropomorphic".

Breton's representation of the Great Transparents is that of beings of a nature and a dimension (or possibly of a number of dimensions) radically beyond human comprehension, just as ants cannot conceive of what human beings are.

Matta's conception is very different... What he identifies as an example of Grand Transparent is rather the ants' communication system, a system that models their interactions, gives shape, and conditions the very existence of the anthill, therefore providing the basis of the existence of ants as a species itself. He gives other illustrative examples such as the Hertzian wave system, or the dynamic conformation of winds in cyclones.

In other words, Matta's vision is rooted in representations of scientific origin (and attempts to go beyond them) while that of Breton, for whom the notion of myth was a central concern at the time, remains more of a " mythological " nature.

In the chapter that follows, I have chosen to use the language of "possession" extensively. Not at all, of course, for religious reasons, nor for reasons related in any way to what is called Occultism, on the contrary. The aim of this text is to take the associated phenomena out of the realms of esotericism and religions and to show that this is a normal and important characteristic of the human mind.

But the use of the vocabulary of possession allows me to attempt a genealogy, a genesis of how the human brain has worked, say since ... "The dawn of time", and the way it has evolved.

It seems to me that the basic functioning of the human mind must have remained largely the same since the appearance of Sapiens, and indeed it does not appear to have undergone any noticeable biological changes. So what makes the difference between hunter-gatherer thinking and our own, are the artifacts (images, ideas, tools) that we have created over the history of the species. Artifacts that we haunt as much as they haunt us.

In what follows, it may also seem that the scope is restricted to the "technical" dimension of things. However, it would be erroneous to remain with this impression because on the one hand, it is essentially meant as an example of a much more general situation, and on the other hand, because from the point of view from which these pages are written, there is no essential difference between the different types of artefacts with which - and thanks to which - we live, be they images, ideas, tools, or even scientific models. So that it would be useless to discriminate between so-called abstract things (images, ideas, models) and so-called concrete things (tools, machines, technologies, and implementation of technical procedures).

Readers who could be bothered by the terminology of "possession" may replace it with "mental simulation". Unless you really believe in "spirits", it doesn't seem to me that there may be a need to make a difference. In fact, the experience of the shaman mainly seems to differ from ordinary human experience by the conscious and deliberate choice of the shaman to implement a particularly passionate and intense mental exploration of the world. In a way, because his own unconscious is both the tools as well as the very object of his quest, the shaman is probably, and by far, more aware of what is going on in his own unconscious than the civilized "man in the street" may possibly be.

The dance of mind and things

In a way perhaps not so far from this automatic gestural writing of Butoh dancing, in an impetus made as much of passion as of abandonment, in terms of imagination of the matter, there had always been the beard of Gaston Bachelard over my shoulder. However , more recently, a friend, by a sort of happy inadvertence, pointed out to me the work of Malcolm de Chazal...

> "Since water is totally relaxed and since, in the same current, none of his gestures is constrained and starched, since water is absolute simplicity, since it is ease itself, and since we cannot simplify what is already the essence of the simple, to "discover" the water, we must hence find something else. And this other thing - this essential condition - is to *add* to water, as one adds a substance to another substance to provoke a reaction and to "reveal" it. And this reagent, added to water to discover it, is yourself that you incorporate into the soul of water, in the following manner. The man who sees a watercourse running will forget after a while that he is himself, and he will gradually feel like the water flowing - making the gestures of the water itself, like the lover abolishes himself in the beloved face and thinks and acts the slightest gesture of her face until he disappears in the life of another, engulfed and melted into her substance. This

integration, which is quite the opposite of narcissism, will soon make us "think water", "act water", "live water", putting us inevitably little by little in another vase of knowledge, on another plane of life, on another degree of consciousness... "

Malcolm de Chazal - *La Vie Filtrée* Pages 88-89 - Collection Imaginaire Gallimard - Gallimard 1949

This page by Malcolm de Chazal, goes further than Surrealism. There is a deep link with Butoh and the experiences of possession that are part of Butoh, without really being part of surrealism, which most often addresses possession only from the outside. Malcolm de Chazal's text can also be related to the myths and associated songs in which two wizards vie in magic and imagination by transforming themselves each one in turn, successively into animals, plants or other different things and beings.

Not only can we find in Malcolm de Chazal certain aspects of the possession phenomena that are part of Butoh, but it turns out that in De Chazal's text, they are also linked to dance ...

"All the gestures of nature can be summed up in a dance movement. [...] Thus, every movement given to water makes the first dance come alive, first of all as a whole - the first dance already existing as principle-essence in water, being the starting point of the form of the Informed. So the dance movement in the water is twofold: the first dance which, in the Informed, has given a form-essence to it, and the secondary dance

25

> which, like a dance envelope around a
> nucleus-dance , makes the water dance as a
> whole and makes dance again in itself the
> "dance heart" of the water, which is its
> pivotal and initial movement, its primary
> dance... "
>
> Malcolm de Chazal - *La Vie Filtrée* P72-73 -
> Collection Imaginaire Gallimard - Gallimard
> 1949

But we also know that this link between dance and possession is by no means restricted to Butoh nor to De Chazal's perception, but is widely spread among the peoples who were not contaminated by the Abrahamic religions.

And yet, Butoh actually seems to mask something that Malcolm de Chazal rightly points out. And the fact is, that possession is not an exceptional mental state which would only be linked to the always somewhat spectacular movements of trance. Possession is in fact the normal state of Malcolm de Chazal while he is writing. And it is also ours when we read it - to the extent, of course, that we agree to share his state of mind in order to understand what he writes.

Besides, we all have consciously experienced such states of possession when we were children. We all knew then, in all its depth and intensity, this "act as if" which is the core of children games :

> "The child learns much more through his toy
> than through a thousand forms of
> conversation - his toy: this first of the starting

points of his thought, where he first began to inimage and to imagine, because by this limitation of his visual field created by the possessive instinct, the child encloses himself by means of his toy into a restricted field of thought, and, being unable to carry other images in this limited trinket, the child is forced to put something of his own self in his toy and to imagine in very the center of himself, to "transplant" himself inside of his toy, to make constructions of his own mind and of his own self in this closed track of life, a ground suddenly walled against the images of the outside".

Malcolm de Chazal - *La Vie Filtrée* P58 - Collection Imaginaire Gallimard - Gallimard 1949

Malcolm de Chazal here rightly points to an important phenomenon. A phenomenon of critical importance in that it sheds light on the way our minds are gradually constructed. However, certain aspects of his interpretation seem questionable to me ...

The first one is the role or function of what he calls the child's "possessive instinct" in the whole process. He should actually know better and more than he says here, because in the above quotes about water he clearly states, leaving aside narcissism, that the mind, when possessed by the spirit of water, is obviously no longer haunted by himself at all. And even less by any sort of possessive instinct. But rather the opposite.

The second problem raised by De Chazal's interpretation, I believe, is the child's specific need to dive into "a ground suddenly walled up against the images of the outside". If the child has to do this, it is not because he is a child, but quite simply because he is a human being. To the extent that we wish to invest a given object or being by means of our mind, from within ourselves, regardless of our age, we must all dispossess ourselves of the grip of the outside world in order to let ourselves be possessed, "invaded", by the object or being in question. This is also very clear in the previous quote where De Chazal tells us about water.

The third problem that De Chazal's formulation seems to me to pose is: what is the purpose of this game of mental possession that children play in themselves when they are left alone and even when playing with other children? This is such a typical and frequent activity that it must probably perform an important biological function, or at least, from the point of view of human biology. De Chazal sees and does say that the child "learns a lot more by his toy than by a thousand other forms of conversation", but he remains silent on this decisive point: what do children actually learn this way?

My personal answer would be that they don't learn anything specific, except to do what they are doing, which is to let themselves be possessed by things around them, in order to mentally grasp those things and become capable of to anticipate, to guess, the behavior of these things or these beings. While the objects chosen to exercise this kind of skill are irrelevant - "just toys" - the process itself is probably critically important ...

Antiquity of modern practices

A few years ago, on television, a documentary showed hunter-gatherers stalking animals. While some of them, superstitious, tried to obtain the good graces of the local hunt spirits through magical practices, others did not. But all of them were using their abilities to let themselves be possessed by the spirit of the animals they were hunting, in order to guess where their prey was going and where it was hiding.

Since such abilities used to be essential to the survival of mankind for hundreds of thousands of years, we can be sure that they still are essential in our daily lives, in a way that is probably obvious, although concealed.

Things may be made easier to perceive based on a story that I have witnessed in the very realm of logic : software development.

About 15 or 20 years ago, IBM's software development managers decided to respond to the large, unpleasant, potentially dangerous, and above all very costly, number of residual errors left in software. After some investigation, they finally found an effective way to remove errors from newly developed software by setting up what they called an "inspection system".

The process consisted of having the software code proofread by several programmers to identify problems and errors. By recording the number of errors found per thousand lines of code and performing statistics based on this recorded data, IBM proved that these inspection practices were much more effective in terms of detecting and removing errors than traditional software testing practices .

As the word "inspection" sounded rather unpleasantly to developers' ears, these practices were later renamed "Peer Reviews," a wording more common in scientific research and publishing.

The company I was working for at the time decided to implement the same type of peer review process. But the average number of defects detected through peer reviews per thousand lines of software source code in our company was well below the figures reported by IBM. So we asked former IBM engineers who had turned consultants to investigate why we were performing so poorly.

After a few hours spent studying our practices, the American consultants finally told us that we had to mentally or even loudly state the text of our software, interpret it, a bit like in a theater play. Otherwise the effectiveness of our defect detection process by means of peer reviews would remain poor and and our efforts almost useless.

As I already knew at that time how hunters in hunter-gatherer groups used to proceed when stalking their prey, my personal conclusion (kept secret) was that we had to reach the point where we would feel, to some extent, inhabited, *possessed*, by our software code.

Any software developer, and even any engineer in the design of complex systems, knows that when stuck with a problem or a bug, the best way out is to describe the problem in loud voice in front of a friend or colleague, and, when possible, while making a number of diagrams on a blackboard. In fact, the colleague you have chosen for this does not need to listen to what you say nor to look at your diagrams at all. Actually, it turns out to be quite unnecessary. However, at the end of less than half an hour of vehement gestures made in front of the total void of attention opposed to you by your very indifferent colleague, you generally find the solution to a problem that had nevertheless been bothering you for a week or two. An this, simply because your friend, who was only minding his own business while waiting for you to finish your little theater scene, kindly served you as a virtual audience. Such is the power and wisdom of possession ...

Generality of mental simulation

Long before peer reviews were introduced into software development teams, developers intuitively knew that mentally interpreting the text of their programs was a prerequisite for them to expect these programs to perform properly. That's why it's not that uncommon to hear a software developer speak out loud when working in a place where he knows - or thinks - to be alone.

And if you have developed an attentive ear to this type of phenomenon, and happen to observe some technicians at work, you will quickly realize that anyone of them, when faced with a somewhat difficult technical problem, will attempt to get out of the situation by trying to characterize in himself, in a low voice or even aloud, the problem that resists him. And I still haven't even said anything about the gestures that often accompany this spontaneous mode of expression when a little geometry in space comes into play with the difficulties encountered.

Instructed by Malcolm de Chazal, I would say that in such a situation people are trying to let the problem come into themselves - another formulation of the same spontaneous phenomenon of willful possession.

We will find similar behavior when observing someone who tries to convince himself of the validity of a non-trivial mathematical proof. This, although mathematics are (somewhat quickly, by the way) generally regarded as the quintessential domain of self-conscious rationality.

Even more commonly, "learning something by rote" involves the same mechanisms and, expressing and repeating within ourselves the things we want to remember, either aloud or silently, is usually required in some way.

On the basis of so general observations, one may think that such phenomena occur (albeit silently or even unconsciously) whenever a human being is confronted with the use of a tool, a machine, or more generally when faced with a "material" or "intellectual" task which has not yet become an automatic process. As humans, it seems that the only approach we have to anticipate what can happen when we use a technical object (and all of the things around us are technical objects, including a good deal of the pathways that our thoughts follow) is - so to speak - to let the "spirit" of this technical object enter into us, or to, ourselves, "mentally enter" into this technical object. Therefore, since our daily human environment is mainly made up of technical objects - be it only forks, knives and spoons - this means that this sort of conscious, or much more often unconscious, "theater of possession" is always active somewhere in our brain. In other words, we mentally "simulate" our environment (technical or otherwise) all the time.

However, the scope of the hypothesis just stated should be restricted because it only applies to tasks which have not yet become automatisms. It is now well known that once a behavior has become an automatism, it migrates to what is commonly called the procedural memory, which is a type of unconscious memory in the sense that we no longer need to call on our little "theater of possession" to walk, talk, swim or ride a bike, all things the learning of which however originally required a large dose of attention.

Procedural memory

If any somewhat complex implementation of technical objects in the course of our daily life always involves a preliminary simulation stage, meant to allow us to predict the result of our actions, this simulation stage can be conscious or unconscious, or even apparently absent when it comes to actions that have almost become of the order of a reflex. But we can imagine that in general, there is no clear line between conscious and unconscious in procedural or technical matters.

As for the procedural unconscious, the situation is very different from what takes place in the field of the Freudian unconscious, where repression prevents certain unconscious elements from coming back to consciousness. Of course, the same repression phenomena may also occur in the domain of the procedural unconscious memory when traumatic events are historically intimately associated with the learning or the implementation of certain procedures of a technical nature.

But it is easy to understand why there must be continuity or gradation between the technical conscious and the technical unconscious. Indeed, although a large part of our actions are performed automatically (such as walking, pressing a switch to turn on the light, for instance), as soon as things become more complex or do not go as planned, our *attention* must take over.

It seems to me preferable to speak here of *attention* rather than of consciousness because, for reasons the religious or at best the philosophical origin of which cannot be in doubt, too much attention has been paid to consciousness, conceived as being a specifically human characteristic which, in animals would be totally or almost totally lacking.

The use of the term attention instead of consciousness, on the other hand, makes it possible to account for the fact that the attentiveness of many animals can be easily observed, and leaves little room for doubt, even for the most hardened religious and philosophers. To consider, for example, that the attention of a predator on its prowl might not be strongly mobilized, would indeed be an evidence of a bad faith that would be difficult to accept.

Mirror neurons

For a long time, possession phenomena were most often associated with trance or the effects of drugs that often accompany it. As spectacular as such things may be, Malcolm de Chazal is undoubtedly closer to the truth when he insists on what he calls *Instinctive Imitation*, which he identifies with what he calls "duplication" or "splitting". Besides, perhaps is the word "splitting" more precise and adequate than the word "possession" because a possessed person does not necessarily cease to be herself, she is often only "partly" possessed, or possessed only intermittently.

> "Instinctive imitation. [...] By this law of instinctive imitation, such a man, for example, will unconsciously imitate such other individual with whom he lives in community, some powerful could be his own personality - personality that the other in return will imitate with as much strength as his will be weak - the strongest here being made more and more imitate than he imitates, the imitation going in the direction and in the regions of least resistance of the personality and inscribing his imprint all as much in the physical as in the moral or in the spiritual from the gestures of the body to the movements of the expression, from the mentality to the mood, from the tastes to the habits, imprinting its seal throughout the field of the activities and the thought of man.

Without this law of instinctive imitation, there would be no society, no country, no nation, for individuality, already pressed enough by the interest, would overflow everywhere and swallow everything. Instinctive imitation is the cohesive force of human societies. "

Malcolm de Chazal, Ibidem P117

As in all comparisons between strong and weak, better or worse, fit or not fit, etc. we must ask ourselves the question of the contexte and of the scale used. And Malcolm de Chazal does not provide any details here. Does a rose's "strength" lie in its scent, colors, resistance to drought or temperature changes, or even in the length of time it flowers? To ask the question is to answer it: it all depends on the considered context and on the points of view.

I shall therefore leave this relative mode of thinking and focus on what is less relative, namely the kind of *instinctive imitation* that De Chazal is talking about here. Although observations of this nature are relatively easy, common, and many people made them long before De Chazal did, we now know that they are no longer just intuitions requiring a degree of sensitivity and subtlety to which De Chazal has accustomed us, but that it is now science. And a science that De Chazal could not know at the time when he wrote La Vie Filtrée (1949), since *mirror neurons* were only discovered in the 1990s by Giacomo Rizzolatti.

Here is, as an indication, what can be found on this subject in the French version of Wikipedia ...

Mirror neurons are a category of neurons in the brain that exhibit activity both when an individual performs an action and when observing another individual (especially of their species) performing the same action, or even when imagining such an action, hence the term "mirror". They are known to be the cause of yawning propagation. There are also echo neurons.

In cognitive neuroscience, mirror neurons are thought to play a role in social cognition, especially in learning by imitation, but also in affective processes, such as empathy. Professor Ramachandran calls them empathic neurons.

Mirror neurons are considered a major discovery in neuroscience. If, for some researchers, they constitute a central element of social cognition (from language to art, including the emotions and understanding of others), for others, these conclusions remain very hypothetical as to the role of these neurons in these psychological processes. The role of these neurons for human social cognition would thus have been greatly overestimated.

There is no need here to discuss in detail the exact role of mirror neurons in "social cognition" given the vagueness that seems to be connected with this expression and the immense field it seems to try to designate ... It's enough to note that the existence of mirror neurons provides a biological basis for what Malcolm De Chazal identifies as "instinctive imitation". As for the rest, the sciences of the mind are by no means finished and if the existence of mirror neurons were sufficient to account for all aspects of human cultures, researchers could devote the rest of their lives to permanent holidays.

Still as an indication, because the function of an encyclopedia in general, or that of Wikipedia in particular, is not to provide the public with a state of the most recent research, but more simply to enlighten the public in order to allow them to go further if desired, let's continue examining the Wikipedia article ...

> The identification of mirror neurons during the 1990s is due to the team of Giacomo Rizzolatti, director of the department of neurosciences at the Faculty of Medicine of Parma.
>
> They were first observed in the ventral premotor cortex of the rhesus macaque monkey (area F5) but also, subsequently, in the rostral part of the inferior parietal lobule. This type of neuron has also been found in some birds where they are activated both when singing and when the animal listens to a singing congener.
>
> In humans, since April 2010 there has been direct evidence for the existence of mirror neurons. Until then, given the many homologies between the brains of different primates, it was accepted that such neurons must also exist in the human species. In addition, by functional brain imaging

(positron emission tomography or functional magnetic resonance imaging, for example), it is possible to observe in certain regions of the cerebral cortex (especially around the Broca area, homologous to the area F5 of the monkey, and at the level of the lower parietal cortex) an activation both when the individual produces an action and when he observes another individual performing a more or less similar action. But, given the spatial resolution of these techniques, there was nothing to confirm that these activations came from exactly the same neurons and not from two populations of intermingled neurons. As a precaution, therefore, the terms "mirror system" or "mirror neuron system" were sometimes used rather than "mirror neurons" to designate these functional areas.

What seems to be problematic in this part of the wikipedia article is determining the precise location of mirror neurons. This "geographical" point of view may perhaps be of interest, but it can be legitimately assumed that, like many other properties of the brain, the mirror effect is probably not a property of individual neurons or even a property of particular assemblies of neurons, but an emerging property of mirror neural *networks*. By emergent property, we mean here a property which makes sense and can only be correctly described at the level of a *network*, and which is not deductible from the individual properties of the components of the network themselves, in this case, neurons. This remark may seem all the more relevant as it seems that, at least in part, these are the same neurons that participate in both real motor actions and simulated motor actions caused by the observation of a congener. In other words, the mirror effect consists precisely in the fact that the activation of the same neurons within different networks can lead either to effective actions or to simulated actions and the question whether a neuron or a group of neurons is of the "mirror" type or not does not make much sense.

What does make sense, however, is that what we know about mirror networks, allows us to understand that the term "possession" - which is, after all, only a form of excessive empathy - is not inappropriate, since mirror neurons are in reality a true "embodiment" of the activity and "mind" of others within ourselves. "Spirit" being taken here in the strict sense of what animates the other (but soul - anima - in its old and original sense would perhaps be more appropriate).

The fact that imitation of the other is not necessarily limited to members of the same species (animal or human) is particularly noticeable among us as primates, since it is generally accepted that monkeys... Ape. But it can also be observed intermittently in our domestic species, for example in the propagation of yawning between species.

On the other hand, there is no doubt that animals can learn by imitation. It's even one of the best ways they learn. In the processes used to teach parrots new knowledge, it was customary to place a (human) master in front of a student, a parrot (usually a Gabonese grey parrot), with the master repeating his lesson in front of the parrot until the parrot learns it. This method worked, but it was not very effective.

The new procedures now consist of placing another animal (usually a human) next to the parrot you want to teach something, with the (human) teacher teaching the same to both students, the human one and the parrot one. With this new way of doing things, the parrot learns by imitation, with this difference, however, that the parrot no longer imitates the teacher, but the human pupil and, when it plays the game with a certain passion, the parrot sometimes manages to give the correct answer faster than the human student.

But Malcom de Chazal pushes his conception of instinctive imitation a little further and generalizes it to contexts where mirror neurons can no longer be called into question, because they do not exist, or not necessarily.

> "Kingdoms and species are complements of each other - the latent forces of other kingdoms and species causing each particular unit of nature to imitate in some degree the species with which it lives in community and which it collides with."

> Malcolm de Chazal - Ibidem P118

And De Chasal is not wrong insofar as nature does not lack phenomena of mimicry; animals imitating their mineral environment (eg octopus) or plant (eg stick insects) or other animals (eg non-dangerous animals imitating dangerous animals to ward off predators - or Batesian mimicry), plants imitating animals (eg orchids imitating the belly of a female bumblebee to attract male bumblebees), plants imitating other plants (passiflores imitating the leaves of other plants to escape the mandibles of caterpillars of their predatory butterflies). All these mimicry are a striking illustration of the propensity of living things, even the unconscious ones, to imitate their mineral environment or other forms of life.

From this perspective, mirror neurons are in fact a special case within a set of much more general "imitation" phenomena.

What is at stake here is not a variety of teleology in which we would interpret a phenomenon of natural imitation according to specifically human intellectual criteria "fallen from Heavens", but the reverse. It is our human intellectual criteria which are the result of biological evolution and, in the case of mirror networks - which are at least one of the bases of our intellectuality - of a tendency of life to imitate which, having proven itself, was selected many times in the course of evolution, until its systematization in the particular case of neural networks.

However, Malcolm de Chazal generally centers his discourse on the "psychic" aspect of instinctive imitation in humans, showing that in the human species, instinctive imitation is by no means reduced to the animal and intraspecific human domains ...

"But besides imitation of plants by animals, there is also imitation of plants by humans. But here the imitation is less direct. It is psychic, participating in the faculty of "duplication" or "splitting". Because in fact, what makes so many narrators believe that the forest comes to life, is that they have it in themselves ; a feeling that the child feels at the highest point, who, being still virgin in the world, is closer to instinct than us and integrates with Nature. "

Malcolm de Chazal - Ibidem, P119

Generally speaking, we tend to place too much emphasis on intentionality. The reasons for this attitude are obviously rooted in religious conceptions that our civilizations still cannot extricate themselves from. Without notions of "fault" or "sin" which are based on intentionality, religions would largely lose their influence. But also ... the courts and the whole judicial system which also feed on the alleged general intentionality of human acts.

It is said that in primitive people everything has a magical cause, and that there are no accidents nor accidental deaths. We show at all times a comparable blindness in that we always stubbornly seek for some responsibilities for everything. Wherever magical intentionality was supposed to account for human events, in our world, the magic disappeared of course, but intentionality remained.

So that, a century after Freud, intentionality is still not questioned. It is confusedly known that *the ego is not the master in its own house*", but everyone nevertheless continues to pretend the ego still rules. Whether this may be considered so for practical reasons, may be acceptable. But the "neural sciences" themselves seem to have as their central objective the elucidation of what consciousness might well be. As if consciousness were the most important thing in the world... As if consciousness could come out of the brain "with helmet and weapons" as Minerva did out of Jupiter's skull, or "naked" as truth comes out of the well. Although it is known that "nothing makes sense in biology except in the light of evolution", we persist in studying consciousness in itself, without paying much attention to the evolutionary circumstances that may have promoted its emergence. Could not it be read in a popular science journal a few years ago, that some claimed to have established that consciousness was based on the activity of one single neuron in the brain and that they had discovered precisely which one! As it stands, the most operational and effective definition of consciousness may almost be considered as being one of the best fundraising vehicles for journalists and many researchers.

But let's come back to a little more reasonable considerations. The question that arises is whether this instinctive imitation that De Chazal speaks of, by which human beings are able to imitate, internalize or, more precisely, mentally model almost everything, systematically corresponds to an activity of mirrors networks. or to those of other types of neural networks.

And here I prefer to use the term modeling rather than the more usual terms of imagination or representation, as these last two terms have a rather static connotation, while the term modeling refers to the dynamic and behavioral aspects that are always integrated in the memory patterns that our brains are constantly building, reusing and improving. And it may well be that at least some of the dynamic aspects of memory are provided by our mirror networks or other similar operations.

Modeling allows simulation, and since our brain does not import real objects in our head for good, since it records the dynamics, and relies on it to act, we can say that our brain simulates.

However, it would be inappropriate and above all, wrong, to say of a shaman that he is simulating, in this flat sense that he claims to be the spirit that possesses him. He's not pretending. He's not doing a show. His purpose is not to impress the public. No, *he is just trying*. He puts himself in a position to explore the unknown

Just as a modern scientist runs a simulation on a computer from a model he has designed, so too does the shaman, except that the computer is himself and that what the shaman simulates, is the particular model of the spirit by which he is possessed, as well as the interactions between this external spirit and his own. And just as the result of a computer simulation is not known in advance - otherwise the simulation would not be undertaken - the result of the act of voluntary possession to which the shaman lends himself is fraught with all the uncertainties of life. Because the Spirit, as they say, blows where it wants. Another way of saying, as Mallarmé pointed out so well, that all thought is woven from chance.

The mental imprint of tools

We must admit that being haunted, inhabited by the world as I hope to have suggested that we are, is probably not without consequences. The human world is populated with spirits, populated with things and living beings that surround it, as ancient and distant mythologies demonstrate to us, as well as the art objects and / or rituals that haunted them. In a time when technical objects were much rarer and (although very sophisticated) much less complex, human brains were more populated with natural objects than today, so they mainly incorporated living things, animals and plants, some singular places and ... of course, already, many other kinds of abstract spirits.

The rapid depletion of usable local ecological resources caused by any somewhat prolonged stay of a group of men – however small – has forced hunter-gatherers, not to starve – as economic theorists believed – but almost always to a certain nomadism. (Cf Marshal Sahlins "Stone Age Economics"). However, nomadism, before the domestication of animals, rests on the shoulders of men and probably even more on the hips of women, which drastically limits to the strict minimum the number of technical objects that one can take with oneself. So that technical development, as sophisticated and subtle as it already was at the time, was thus also quantitatively limited.

The world in which we have lived since the Neolithic is very different. The domestication of animals and the establishment of agriculture allowed much more comfortable forms of nomadism in most cases, and true sedentarization in just about all others. Circumstances which favored accumulation, not only of food in granaries or on horses and camels' backs, but also the accumulation of all kinds of technical objects from art, crafts and trade.

So even though plants, animals and singular places continued to haunt the minds of men, they did so in very different ways... Whereas hunters among hunter-gatherer peoples sometimes used to apologize to the spirits of their prey before or after killing them, Neolithic peoples behaved very differently towards their cattle.

Because cattle are the *animal-tool*. And the tools... We make them, we take them, we give them, we forget them or we throw them away when we consider that they are no longer usable, or that they are encumbering us. Tools, we have the right to use and abuse them, as the Roman laws on property used to say. So with the cattle too, but with a little moderation however, since that's what we eat.

With the Neolithic, technical objects, including animals and plants, are there when you want them to be, and are no longer there when you no longer want them to be there. *The world has become deterministic...* Whereas in a hunting and gathering economy, the tools are always too heavy, the animals do what they want, and the plants only do good gatherings when they want as well.

The slave, can only appear when the population increases, when the inter-group distances are reduced and the surrounding strangers become inevitable, and as a consequence, war too. The slave is the *man-tool* or rather, more frequently the woman-tool. The slave as such is not incompatible with the hunting-gathering economy, but the slave must be fed and ecology once again imposes its limits on the size of groups. While a slave may not be unfit for picking, it is a bit trickier to send him, armed, into a forest to hunt for you. And if, being nomads, you have no desire to encumber yourself with slaves that you will have to watch constantly in all your movements, then you may think of eating your slaves. But once you have done it, there are no more slaves left.

So much so that with the Neolithic, almost the entire universe, plants, animals, earth and men were transformed into technical objects. So that the souls, that is, the independent spirits that were supposed to animate the corresponding wild things, gradually disappeared - of human brains at least.

Everything that was little or not at all manipulable in the world of hunter-gatherers became daily manipulable in the Neolithic world. Of course, we continued to respect the spirit of some animals, and until today we still find lions, tigers, bulls, hawks and eagles, oaks and olive trees, on emblems, on money coins, in logos, on cars and of course on flags. But this is only allegorical. The heart and the passion are gone, and the magic is gone too.

However, while it can still sometimes happen to a

man to walk naked, we can be sure, on the other hand, that no man has ever walked with an empty mind. So that the spirits of animals, plants and more generally the spirits of nature having deserted men's minds, they had to be filled with other things.

What's in a man's mind?

Well no... This is *not* an image of a man's mind.

But, if we assume the structure of the unconscious is similar to that of a language, perhaps questioning language will open doors for us towards the unconscious – at least towards the collective aspects of the unconscious.

A cavalier analysis of a thesaurus of about 350 words and expressions designating the masculine sex in the French language gives the following results:

• 46% of terms and expressions related to technical objects or technology (including war technology)

• 14% of terms and expressions related to animals or plants (eg: anaconda, eel, asparagus ...)

• 9% of terms and expressions linked to names or first names of characters (eg Adam, Adolf, Jack, Freddy ...)

n• 4% of culinary terms (ex: nem, nouille, andouille, ...)

• 4% of adjectives used as nouns (eg huge, inexorable, indomitable, painful,...)

• 3% of diminutives (eg zizi, zigounette, zezette, ...)

The set of the terms thus analyzed represents approximately 80% of the considered thesaurus .

Even taking into account classification errors or misinterpretations, it must be admitted that the collective unconscious linked to the male sex seems quite strongly marked by technology and that, if human beings seem somewhat obsessed with sex, it appears that the male sex itself seems somewhat obsessed with tools and work ...

Now, what about the terms and expressions used to designate the female sex?

The analysis of a thesaurus of approximately 270 words and expressions designating the female sex in French gives slightly different results:

• 28% of words from the technical world - including religious. (for example ring, doors, jewelry, altar, mortar, ...)

• 22% of words related to animals or plants (eg: broccoli, beaver, cat, crayfish, elephant, etc.)

• 11% of diminutives (ex: choupette, chounette,

conelet, conillon, frifri, mimi, minette, monette, puppoune, foufoune ...)

• 6% of geographical or geological terms and expressions (for example cave, mountain, stream, ...)

• 2% culinary terminology (eg: escalope, puff pastry, honey jar, hair pie, etc.)

• 1% of qualifiers used as nouns (for example, slobbery, bearded, ...)

All the terms thus analyzed cover approximately 70% of the thesaurus considered.

Again, the frequency of technical terminology – on condition of course that care is taken to extend it to the field of house technical objects, of architecture or of the religious context – is not negligible, although less striking than in the male sex case. It roughly corresponds to the percentages of occurrences of associated with plants and animals if we add it to occurrences of geographic or geological terminology.

Of course, the considered thesauri, chosen at random on the Internet, are arbitrary, as can be in some cases the choice in the classification process. However, it would probably be difficult to find equivalent amounts of technical terms designating sex among hunter-gatherer peoples such as some pygmies, some aborigines of Australia or some "bushmen" of South Africa.

Yet isn't it surprising to find so many "civilized" technical terms in a context that religions have so often described as the very locus of animality?

What the vocabulary suggests, sadomasochistic imagery confirms it. We can almost certainly identify sadomasochism with the presence of objects that slip between bodies: ropes, whips, costumes, torture chambers, erotic meals, decors that look like workshops, automobiles, fantasies of slavery, complex postures and sometimes quasi-architectural body asemblies, as in Sade's writings, etc. Even more than in the expressions of pain, so outwardly similar to those of pleasure, in sadomasochism we are in a workshop. In a workshop and sometimes almost in a factory, as in Sade imaginations, for example, where the excitement of pure numbers sometimes reaches a kind of passion.

The sadomasochistic theater, although secretly governed by the rules of the contract, likes to be taken seriously and wants to be. That of men, above all. In this regard, erotic shops for men are very different from those frequented by young women since such shops now exist to make their dreams float.

In men's boutiques, you really feel like you're in a theatrical props store where every object strives to look realistic. A goal that it usually does not achieve, and which somewhat annihilates the dark imprint of seriousness with which it would like to be adorned. So you usually have to take a little mental trouble to "believe in it".

The opposite is true in women's boutiques, where the playful atmosphere of sparkling pink and rhinestones gives them an air of joy and where objects and utensils are undeniably aimed more at the elegance of curves and aerodynamics than at realism. It's another game, quite different. The lack of seriousness is complete, and from a certain point of view, from a male's point of view, almost ... unseemly. Girls are probably more playful than we are, which may sometimes seem slightly depressing to us.

Still, both places have technical colors, and desire, whether dark or solar, is crossed by objects.

Child games

Sometimes I happen to remember our games in the playground when I was four or five years old. I particularly remember two of them. We used to dig holes in the gravel bed that covered the ground of the courtyard, we squatted on them and, very convinced and imbued with the seriousness of our actions, we incubated imaginary eggs. I guess some of us invented this game by observing the hens from the surrounding farms.

But we also had other, more technically colored, game schemes, which consisted of running around the playground with outstretched arms, whirring at the best. We were imitating the planes from the neighboring American base, of which we embodied the various plane models that we could see passing over our heads. The ones that impressed us the most were the "two tails", twin-fuselage planes that seemed very strange to us and for which we had a special quality of devotion.

I'm not used to visiting playgrounds anymore, but I heard some years ago that the games have changed there. Now kids are "programming" each other. One sits behind his friend's back and types on his overcoat – momentarily transformed into an imaginary keyboard – instructions that the other hastens to execute once the final "enter" key is pressed.

Ever since these memories came back to me, with the associated words and gestures, I can't help but think that adults in their sadomasochistic games are a lot like those children who play at becoming things or manipulating other children who have temporarily decided to become things. This led me to consider the "dramatic" aspects of sadomasochistic theaters from a different angle from the ones from which they are still often seen. I mean, I look at them with an amused eye, often with a tinge of humor but ultimately a rather tender view.

It's hard to imagine when these mask games that we play with our things could have been introduced. They are probably as old as the existence of the masks themselves. But it seems to me that they reveal the duplicity of our things, which are *from us*, and which *are us* in a way, although *without being us* and with which we have been buried for a long time, sometimes with our women, our horses and our slaves. If our things did not dwell so deeply in us, if they had not reached such a degree of existence in the depths of our minds, why would we attempt to take them with us to the worlds to come? And closer to us, what is a heritage apart from this ballet of things where brothers and sisters sometimes tear each other apart for a trinket?

I also remember an episode when I was still a teenager, digging the ground in the garden. I was quite proud of myself, the sporty soul and almost Stakhanovist, because I had dug a fairly large piece of land, and confusedly, more or less consciously, I felt almost as powerful and radical as a big mechanical digger. And then my mother came along with a whole different mindset, and she broke my courageous momentum. "You know," she said, "you have to pluck and remove the roots, otherwise what you're doing is useless because the weeds will grow back".

No ! It had been quite exciting to embody a beautiful machine for a moment, and now my mother came to remind me of the boring and vaguely unworthy condition of being human ... Not even speaking about kneeing once in a while, in order to pull out those damn roots. I suddenly stopped and put the spade aside. But my mother was wrong. She came from a definitely old-fashioned and vanishing world. I've never seen anyone worry about removing weed roots when people use a tiller.

However, I can still very well see my father, a retired schoolteacher, son of peasants and really not very rich ones, and who was then 80 years old, almost removing the tiller from my hands, and tracing furrows with the most thoughtful, serious and convinced air, and who above all took a loving care of his "tournailles", the piece of land that can only be plowed at the end, because it is the place which is reserved for turning the plow in order to start plowing the next furrow in the other way. I don't think the noise and the rather relative power of the engine moved him much, but I think it would have been a great pleasure for him to put a horse in front of the tiller. He did not embody the engine but the plowing. Perhaps in those moments, had he become for a moment the plow itself! Other technology, other dreams ...

We don't always imagine how deeply the soul of

things can nestle in us ... Not long ago, in math lessons, a lot of children didn't want straight lines to "cut each other" as the French say (intersect). They all had pocket knives at the time and what usually happens in such cases had of course happened to them: wounds, blood, smell of ether, stinging alcohol, compresses, band-aid and all the stuff. In short, a sort of frightening disaster for a child. And it was these memories that made straight lines abstract, aggressive, dangerous, and in short, unbearable for them. Since those dark and remote times, the world has changed. In math lessons, straight lines no longer intersect but gently "meet". It feels a little bit better. Even though math classes have remained pretty much what they already were in those dark and remote times: a disaster.

Nonetheless, I do not personally use the word "section" without some vague apprehension.. Reasonable as I am, I of course casually dismiss the word with a swift movement of my mind. Yet, as for the word "vivisection", it is not for nothing in the root causes for which I did not become a doctor but a computer scientist. Silicon doesn't bleed, especially when you don't really need to touch it too much.

We must at all times embody our tools, our things, imitate them, model our relationships with them, let them haunt us to some extent, in order to anticipate the consequences of their use and avoid accidents. Just as we do with animals and other human beings actually. It doesn't always happen smoothly, or without difficulty, nor sometimes without trauma.

Feedbacks

But all this is not without return effects either. What happens is, so to say, that the shadow, the spirit, of our tools and of our things haunt us, consciously of course, as we most often think when we get aware of it, but above all unconsciously, although we oddly forget to think about such a possibility. The use of our tools and of our things changes us, transforms our brain, and of course our relations with the human world and more generally with the non-technical world.

On the one hand, we have to consider our tools and our things, to some extent, as alter egos, in order to be able to imitate them, to mimic them. But on the other hand our short-term vision, our *realism*, push us not to accept this situation. Our ordinary realism tells us to reduce them to what we believe they are, to what they are meant to be, simple functional, familiar, and therefore dominated beings (since "domus" originally means the family home). Realism stands entirely in this formula: "*this* is **just** *that*".

We therefore tend to stick to the visual evidence that a tool or a thing is only this object which stands in front of us, which corresponds moreover to the etymology of the word "object", which comes from the Latin "objectum" : "that which is placed before or in front." The obviousness of this object thrown before our eyes, almost immediately makes us lose all awareness that this thing has its roots deeply within us. So deeply indeed that we do not even realize that none of our things makes any sense without those roots that plunge deep into us. And these roots do not only include the "know-how" of the thing, but also incorporate all the dynamics associated with using it : this thing, as well as the mental mimicry associated with this thing, which we will have to interpret as a silent theater play within ourselves if we are to use it correctly and effectively.

Similarly, we do not realize that this thing also has roots in the world outside of it and that it is actually intertwined in a vast network of processes that includes its production, the social environment and the technical environment required to use it, as well as the methods and precautions for storing it, disposing of it safely, or reusing or recycling it.

So is it rather distressing to hear so many people – including many of them who should know more about the nature of Realism – say that their tools (cell phone, computer, etc.) are *just tools*". They are extremely proud to state that they only make use of their phones for phone calls. They bought a refrigerator and they thought it was just a tool to cool their food. They did not realize that it was also a way to destroy the Earth's ozone layer. They bought a car to travel faster and easier, and they thought a car was "just a car", not realizing that it was also a way to send carbon dioxide into the atmosphere and create a greenhouse effect. Tools are just what they want them to be, perfect and obedient slaves. Nothing else than a well identified function.

In the real world, no object can ever be reduced to a function,as it is irrevocably part of Universal History and as such it is and remains open to all hazards. Outside of the human world, nothing in the Universe has a function. And even within the human world, the notion of function remains indeterminate at all times, for it is constantly subverted by any unforeseen use that can be made of an object.

During one of his lectures, the theoretical biologist Stuart Kauffman asks the public to list all the possible uses of a screwdriver. Hands are raised, proposals are flowing from all sides and the list of possible uses continues to grow...

He then proposes the audience to list all the possible uses of a screwdriver, but this time, of an isolated screwdriver floating in the dark depths of the outer space, even taking into account that a human arm may have been added to the screwdriver for the purpose of activating it. And suddenly in the conference room, the audience remains silent.

This provides the evidence that the function does not reside in the object itself, but in our mind. In our mind, of course, but not only. Because the function also lies in the context. To tell the truth, a function is nothing else than an *encounter,* something of the same order as "the occasion which makes the thief". Of course this type of encounter is highly organized and made repeatable. But if we take a closer look, it appears that a function never really loses that somewhat evanescent, casual, character of an encounter.

The totality of ecological problems is in fact linked to the realist and reductionist phrase according to which "*this is **just** that*", which reduces everything to what we think we know of it.

It should be better known that realism is nothing but a mousetrap. As Nietzsche pointed out in bluntly applying the ordinary refrain of realistic reductionism backwards:

> "The realist painter claims to paint reality, but he never paints anything of it but what he knows how to paint. "

No, "this" is never "just that". The universe is irremediably an adventure to be lived. Or rather, to put it better, the Universe is a living adventure. It is not a place where you can pretend to save yourself a little effort by letting tools and things do the work for you. The real function of technical objects is to allow us to venture further. Not to take away from us the pain of living.

The ecological and social problems which result from the blindness that the realistic attitude carries with itself, show that it is a false and dangerous point of view. We should accept the fact that our tools and our things have some degree of autonomy. Some kind of autonomous life that we are not aware of. We should look at them from an almost animistic point of view (since our technical unconscious animates them anyway and since we cannot escape of that), we should show them some kind of technically educated *respect* as suggested by the French philosopher Gilbert Simondon. It would probably be a much wiser and healthier attitude than to regard them more or less as slaves, as we currently do.

Strictly speaking, an ecological problem is *not* a technological problem. It is what the salesperson did not tell us about what he sold to us, it is what he "forgot" to tell us ("par une étourderie de système" as Fourier said). To reduce a technical object to its identified and listed use, to what it is supposed to do, to what people claim it is doing, is always to take the point of view of the person whose business is to sell it to us.

Besides, a salesperson does not sell us a thing or a tool. He only sells us *ownership* of that thing or tool, not the use of it. Whether we use it or not is not his problem. He doesn't care. He sells you a car, but he doesn't sell you the driver's license, nor the costly driving lessons that go with it. He doesn't sell you the breakdowns nor the traffic accidents, although they are, in fact, an integral part of the car. He doesn't tell you that, in fact, you are not the one driving your car, but that the car is driving you from one gas station to the next gas station. And he also tells you nothing about the wars over access to oil in which you or your children and friends can lose their lives.

Technology and Capitalism

Like any human society type, capitalism is based on technology. But capitalism is by no means the same as technology itself. It makes a very particular use of technology, a specific use which, in fact, excludes the end use of technology, because capitalism is based on exchange value and not on use value.

It has become a very common attitude, and truly almost a routine these days, to condemn technology, thus forgetting that the type of technology we live in is by no means technology "in general", technology "as such", but only a very particular subset of technologies such as they have been selected and adapted to the specific needs of capitalism. *Most particularly to class struggle requirements*. This now extremely common technophobia results both from a deep lack of analysis as to the way in which things, tools and techniques relate to human thought or more precisely to the human brain and body on the one hand, but also, and even above all, from the surprising weakness of the usual analyzes as regards what capitalism really is and what it does with technology on the other hand.

Almost no political analysis of decisions about technological choices that have been made throughout the history of capitalism has been conducted. Why were steam engines, requiring the purchase of expensive coal, preferred over water mills which did not have such associated costs? Why have individual cars been preferred to trams and the extension of rail networks? Etc.

Some still know that Paris was completely rebuilt by Haussman in a way that made it much easier to cope with labor riots. Others recall that the Situationist International made it clear that post-war architecture, and urban planning more generally, had been driven by the need to impose the capitalist political order and by the demands of widespread mental repression. Besides, hadn't Dali hesitated to speak of a "self-punishment architecture"? But since architecture and town planning are notoriously technologies, by what sort of strange intellectual miracle do most people fail to understand that what happened with architecture and town planning happened in the same way to all the decisions that have been made about all the technologies used in the capitalist world?

The point is, that most people's thinking about technology rarely goes beyond the autonomy level achieved by plants. A plant does not have the capacity to move, it must hence adapt to the place where it grows, as if this place were the only one in the world, or else it perishes. On the other hand, when the place where it is does not suit it, an animal knows that there are other places and it moves there. The lack of technological thought leads people to consider that the technology currently deployed is the only one possible, and this for the sole reason that it exists. Like plants, the thought of most of our contemporaries adapts to what is there and is unable to move beyond it.

The depths of the lack of human imagination are decidedly unfathomable ...

Yet, given the ongoing and future ecological problems, it should seem reasonable to undertake a body of studies to identify and critique the technical decisions that have been made by capitalism throughout its history. This, among other reasosns, in order to understand why certain solutions were chosen, what were the other possible solutions, and why they were rejected. This would make it possible to verify whether the technical solutions that were once rejected by Capitalism could possibly be used in a non-capitalist society or not. But this kind of political history of technology is neither undertaken, and indeed, it's not even intellectually conceived.

Depths of the technical imprint

This situation reveals another aspect of how technology has taken hold of men. And this, whether they are "geeks", technically speaking, or whether they are the complete opposite of a "geek", that is to say when they belong to the huge crowd of technophobic people who not only don't realize that their entire lives are built on technology but that they are literally sitting on it. (Yes. A simple chair is also a technical object!).

We have now come to the point where technology haunts our minds to such an extent that we are caught in the false alternative of two opposing positions, that are either to be fans of what is there, or to reject all of it.

It sounds a lot like the kind of particularly stupid and sterile binary opposition that had become almost universal during the Cold War era. You had to be either a follower of capitalism or a follower of "communism", with no possible acceptable escape. Those times are over, but while people have finally recognized the contrived and fictitious nature of such a binary opposition, that hasn't stopped them from happily jumping into the next one.

Another striking aspect of how technology has taken hold of men is that you regularly hear people complaining about the huge mess and the immense amount of garbage that has accumulated all around them. However they don't seem to be able to realize, that this mess and garbage has only one origin: the human brain – And yes ! Theirs included.

Yet the point is, the human brain is bound to contain the same kind of mess, clutter, and garbage as the environment outside the brain. And even much worse, because the monstrous mental dumping ground that has been growing in our brains and which now controls our behaviors, not only includes what was actually produced, but also what could have been produced, what could not be produced, as well as everything that was dreamed of, and all that peole once have dreamed of selling.

Another aspect of the situation was highlighted by Günther Anders in *L'obsolescence de l'homme*, with the concept of "Promethean Shame". It is about the feeling which invades the human being - in particular a worker - when he realizes that a machine can carry out much better than himself, more quickly and especially much more economically, the very work which ended up making his pride because he was told that it justified his salary. Suddenly finding yourself equated with a thing, that is, suddenly finding yourself being like a thing, is obviously traumatic, and being fired in the same moment certainly does not help overcoming the crisis.

But the intoxication of human minds by technoloy reaches new heights with certain categories of suicides. A very large number of people are haunted by tools to such a degree that they get completely lost, and come to be overwhelmed with a sense of global absurdity when they suddenly realize that *they are useless*.

They failed to understand, and are even radically incapable of conceiving, that the only things that have any use in the Universe are tools, machines, objects ... These people are so deeply haunted by things and tools, that they come to envy them. *They want to be useful*, they want to have a meaning, they want to *serve*. Serve a cause, serve other people, serve something, whatever it is. It doesn't matter whether it's God or Devil, but *serve*.

And their intellectual foundations suddenly collapse when they realize that neither themselves nor the Universe were ever meant to be of use to anything nor anyone. Their intellectual underpinnings slip away even more drastically when they suddenly realize that neither themselves nor the Universe were ever meant to *mean* anything, were never meant to have a meaning. Having a goal, a meaning, a use, a target, an objective, is a concept that only has meaning within the human world, in the human technological context. But outside of the human world, such concepts do not make sense. And people suddenly realize all of this, and panic when faced by what they call the Absurd and some of them die from this frightening discovery that *they are not things*.

Beyond this nonsense about the Absurd, of which the existentialist philosophers for a time made their money and fame, we must take into account that human brains are located right at the limit, right at the interface, between a useless universe, a useless living nature , and the human technical bubble within which everything has a meaning, a purpose, a goal. Human beings are inseparably natural and cultural. Denying our joint membership in these two worlds leads to this creeping and underlying form of madness that wants everything in the Universe to be there for some reason and to serve some use. It would really be making the world ridiculously small to grant it an existence only in relation to a goal. This would be to reduce the Universe, in short, to a creation, to the production of a "higher" entity - as if God could be "higher than" something, as if his actions could be reduced to the result of some particular intention.

On the contrary, it is the greatness, the immense freedom and the marvelous character of the human condition to be useless, to have no meaning, to be of no use. To stand proudly – and to remain – well beyond any utilitarianism. And to fight daily for that.

Living with images...

Now, just as it is impossible for the human brain not to be haunted by images – would it be the image of a pure and total void, as certain Eastern traditions propose – it is also impossible for the humain brain not to be haunted by things, whether they be material and concrete things or abstract and "intellectual" things. This is how brains work, and who wants to get rid of all images should consider getting rid of their brains. A decision that is usually not taken lightly ...

Yet, while there is no way to escape the world of images, tools and things, there is a way to *live with them* and achieve some kind of *symbiosis*. This means is Poetry. The poet is no less haunted by images than others, but the uniqueness of his approach is that he wants to be. Such is his goal, his work, his art of living. Images are indeed the very object of his research. But because he welcomes them and because he seeks them, in a word because he knows how to *live with them*, the poet is not submitted to images. He is aware of the game that images are playing in his mind. But he plays with images in the same movement in which he know be to be himself played by images.

The poetic process makes the poet aware of the passage and movement of images in the human mind. Where the non-poet – that is, the one who has forgotten that he was a poet – is manipulated by images, precisely because he opposes them, denies their existence and their games, and refuses taking them into account, the poet, on the contrary, lets them enter himself, follows them, to the point of trance if necessary, but in the end he knows them as images and accepts to live with them. He accepts the company of the liquid and erratic moire of images.

Surrealists, that is, poets whose activity consists in studying and collectively implementing "the real functioning of thought", are in the most appropriate position to be aware of the movement of images in their minds. Contrary to what the requirements of the art and literature markets continue to make the public believe, the surrealists were never writers, poets or artists. On the contrary, the surrealist movement can be credited with having put an end to the separations between the various traditional fields of artistic and literary activities.

But on closer inspection, this direction of surrealist activities was in fact nothing else than a return to a kind of *global* intellectual activity that the Renaissance historical period had brilliantly illustrated centuries before. Many of the great Renaissance artists were also engineers, scientists and researchers. Piero della Francesca, now known mainly as a painter, has also been described as the greatest mathematician of his time. Brunelleschi was an architect, but he also invented a few machines, including a paddle-wheel ship to transport marble. Michelangelo was not only a painter, but also an architect. And everyone knows that Vinci did not only paint the Mona Lisa, but that he also invented a good number of machines, that he was an architect, and that he built many automatons to animate the festivals of princes who employed him. It is therefore not by chance that Marcel Duchamp put mustaches on the Mona Lisa - following a Montmartre painter who had represented her smoking a cigarette - but rather in a manner of winking at Leonardo da Vinci whose work he had spent a few years studying at the Bibliothèque Sainte Geneviève in Paris. We can consider Duchamp - but he is not the only one in Surrealism, thus Dali himself - as an heir to the Renaissance.

While some surrealists of the past have been led to consider only the Freudian unconscious, it is very likely that there is a way to gain access to the procedural unconscious as well, even if it is about a type of unconscious so usual and so common that it is completely forgotten, just like the Freudian unconscious was before Freud.

And yet, while we do not remember when and how we learned how to walk, to speak, and while in any conversation we do not even know by what sort of miracle we can manage to pronounce a single word, language has become for us a kind of automatism - although it is not really an automatism since we can use language to say a lot of different things and sometimes we happen to use language in radically creative way. Almost everything has been written on language and the Freudian unconscious, but almost nothing on the relations of language and the unconscious procedural memory which is nevertheless underlying it, and without which we would not be able to pronounce even a single word.

Likewise, riding a bicycle or swimming, or simply using a fork or a spoon to eat, have also long become automatisms. But again, they are not really automatisms, since we can adapt and bend these "automatisms" according to our will, the context and the necessities of the moment.

If we admit that language is really at the heart of what makes us human beings (which I personally doubt), and if, with Lacan we can even come to consider that "the unconscious is structured like a language" (which is debatable), since a language is a tool, and a tool that is structured differently depending on the variçous languages, then it must be the same regarding anything that ends up being sucked into the depths of our unconscious procedural memory. In other words, there must exist a kind of common underpinning between the underlying structures of the various human languages and those which condition and authorize our technical learning.

Thus, for example, it was long thought and affirmed that human language was characterized by "the double articulation". We now know that such ideas were perhaps a little too fast and that some monkeys are able to articulate different usual isolated signals to compose messages adapted to different semantic contexts - even if they do so only in a way that may look, for us a little rudimentary.

But what should attract our attention is precisely the use of the term *articulation* which, in this occurence, comes from the technical vocabulary. From then on, we quickly see that we have known how to articulate our actions, to move, eat, walk ... Long before learning to articulate words, sentences and everything we articulate in language-related objects : paragraphs, chapters, volumes, libraries, etc. Again, this capacity for technical articulation is not specifically human. The New Caledonian crow is able to articulate a technical sequence of three steps including various tools, to achieve its ends. I also remember an article on animal intelligence where a photo showed a chimpanzee standing on top of three boxes trying to grab a banana with a stick, while the neighboring article struggled to demonstrate that animals are incapable to plan ...

Industrial societies are providing all possibles evidences that technologies articulate with each other (or are combined) and that *technology unfolds like a language ...*

All of these skills that we once acquired, and which have become "automatisms", are part of us, and in a way, they *are* us. Or else should we restrict our vision and only consider what we are without them? Which would mean to become something like a newborn baby again. And there is no doubt that we do remain this newborn baby all our life long, and that these still unidentified basic skills, these "lost powers", which are however not lost are those which allow us to learn and go on learning until we die.

What could we learn from a generalized poetic approach which, beyond words and language, would be extended to acts themselves? A new kind of art? A new kind of poetry? Maybe or maybe not. But we shouldn't care, because Surrealism was meant to be an adventure and because art and poetry were never meant to be anything but examples and not what Surrealism was supposed to be restricted to. *"We do not like art nor artists"* said Jacques Vaché.

But, by extending the domain of poetry to the acts themselves and to the "automatisms" which underlie our acts, we could study how human beings learn. How they learn both "physically" and "intellectually", thus transcending for once the age-old division between body and mind. And we could study what kind of roles the unconscious part of ourselves plays in it. Something similar to what Gaston Bachelard did about the historical evolution of scientific concepts, when he created the notion of "epistemological obstacle", and later when he studied what he called "The imaginations of matter". Or, instead of complaining, in the ugliest, laziest, and most passive way, that machines are now able to learn, instead of feeding our minds with ignorant newspaper articles devoted to a so-called deep learning, maybe could we gain something in trying to understand how humans and animals really learn - and much more effectively than artificial neural networks. Perhaps could we venture out to investigate these still largely untouched grounds of conscious and unconscious learning, and play with what we might discover there. It would no longer be essentially a matter of learning something, but rather of learning how we come to learn that something.

At a collective level, in the same way as Vincent Bounoure (Groupe Surréaliste de Paris) and Vratislav Effenberger (Groupe Surréaliste de Prague) and their comrades once moved from individual automatic writing to collective automatic writing, since we know well enough that most of learning is quite likely based on unconscious skills (similar or perhaps the same as in a newborn baby), it would be possible to research how automatic learning might be collective. This would be entirely in accordance with the extension of Surrealism proposed by Bounoure and Effenberger, in *La Civilisation Surréaliste* (1976) when they envisaged encompassing all human activities, i.e. both those falling within the scope of infrastructure (i.e. production and exchange) and those relating to the superstructure (i.e. ideas and representations), and therefore the entire field of human expression, as the legitimate playground of a surrealist civilization.

Not only would such a project fit into the perspective previously proposed by Bounoure and Effenberger, but it would also lead us more or less directly to the unconscious roots of all human activities, intellectual ones or not.

We could then expect to recover the human "lost powers" as has always been one of the goals of Surrealism ... Because, after all, to consider things a little seriously, if the lost human powers are not present at the heart of the paths by which newborn babies learn, unless we accept that they are "falling from Heavens", it is difficult to see where they could possibly originate from.

Besides, there is every reason to believe that the way in which adults and adolescents learn, if one could examine it in depth, cannot be so different from the way in which babies spontaneously learn .

Because, after all, what is learning? It is to progressively build - in fact, to *create*! - a general and reusable abstract form out of a magma of raw perceptions. We must indeed use the term "*create*" here, because nothing proves that the representations that our brain constructs correspond to real objects. And an eviudence of it, is that we are constantly changing and adapting them. Adapting representations is properly called learning, and it is, within us, as with many other animals, a constant activity.

This creation and adaptation of forms is what formal neural networks are today capable of. But they can only reach that, out of a huge number of examples - hundreds of thousands to millions of examples.

Obviously, biological neural networks of most animals - including insects - are much more flexible and more "efficient". Despite the noise made of it, it is rather unlikely that any current artificial neural network will be able to match the intelligence of a simple bee ...

But if we stick to the definition of learning proposed above, we cannot help but make the link with the problem that Matta posed in his *psychological morphologies*, that is to say to try to grasp the dynamics of perception before it fossilizes into a form. But Matta was an essentially visual thinker and very close to Marcel Duchamp's problematic, itself derived from Relativity and the notions of 4-dimensional spaces. Matta approached things from an essentially geometric point of view - albeit multidimensional. In what is here proposed, the target would not only be to study the visual aspects of the learning process, but actually, all aspects of human learning, i.e., in order to express things in absolutely general terms, the way we come into contact with the world and the way the world touches us and penetrates us.

One would have hoped that Matta's successors in the United States, the artists of the art school which became known as Abstract Expressionism, seized on Matta's problematic, like Matta had taken up Duchamp's problematic. But it seems that they mainly took over the appearances of Surrealism, its artistic shell, rather than its spirit. Matta himself, re-using a well-known expression from Rimbaud, ended up characterizing this profound lack of wit in the general attitude of Abstract Expressionisme with the following remark: "The reasoned disruption of all the senses, yes. But *for the meaning* ".

It must also be said that, in the time of the Cold War, when Abstract Expressionism historically flourished, the objective of American governments was to promote the emergence of a "Western" form of art and even more precisely of an "American" Art, in order to make the counterpart of the "Soviet" Realism, and hence rather "Russian" art. Quite a strange idea indeed, that art may have a nationality... But we can say that the maneuver was fully successful in all respects, even if it is not entirely certain that intelligence has gained anything, either in one case or in the other.

The fact remains that the extension of Matta's problematic, which could have been expected for example from *Action Painting*, did not occur in the United States, and that it only partially took place in Northern Europe with movements like CoBrA and under the influence, for example, of the Asger

Jorn's ideas, whose intuitions, like those of Matta, foreshadow the current period.

All in all, the general impression which emerges from the Cold War period is rather disappointing, leaving a feeling of missed opportunities, of sometimes daring experiments but from which it does not seem that many lessons were learned. A general impression which would tend to accede to the opinion that "there is no progress in art", which the Renaissance, and to a lesser extent surrealism itself, yet most strikingly invalidate.

However, the very cavalier description given above of Matta's problematic quickly appears incomplete and even unfair as soon as we consider that Matta's approach was never reduced to the dynamics of the couple raw perceptions versus representation, but that he always sought to extend it to other areas of intellectual activities. It is important to note that it is through this constant concern that Matta indisputably surpasses Duchamp who, strangely enough, does not seem to have taken any interest in it.

Because contrary to what we have now learned from formal neural networks suggests, learning is obviously not limited to a transition between raw perceptions and representation, but there is every reason to think that similar types of transitions occur, through perhaps different or perhaps similar mechanisms, in the different abstraction levels of the domain of ideas and of the dynamics that can be associated with them (in other words, models).

Although what has been developed so far has concerned little more than almost gestural aspects of the unconscious, the point was in fact only a matter of giving an example. It remains just as much to elucidate the way in which ideas emerge from a type of unconscious which does not seem to have very close relations with the Freudian vision of the unconscious, somewhat handicapped by its rather narrowly therapeutic origins. This area of the conscious-unconscious dynamics of ideas has hardly been explored except by mathematicians - and not the least of them : Henri Poincaré and Alexandre Grothendieck most particularly - often attentive to the way ideas emerge in their minds. The rather widespread panic inspired by the simple word Mathematics is undoubtedly responsible for the lack of interest, as astonishing as it is general, associated with the observations of mathematicians. The fact that Mathematics may inspire some fear is understandable, but that such a fear may also extend to the biographical writings of mathematicians themselves is more inexplicable.

The evisceration of langage

However, one thing is to propose the project of a generalized poetry, but it is quite another to achieve such a project to take shape ... Let us consider as an example what is currently happening to language and poetry in the type of social organization where we live ...

The very particular use that is currently made of technology takes us away from any real contact with the world, from *the caress of the world*. In everything that we encounter in our daily life we are *delivered* in a way compliant with the double meaning of the term emphasized by Günther Anders in his book *L'Obsolescence de L'Homme*. We are delivered, of course in the sense that "ready-made" objects are delivered to us, objects which are pure results, that is to say totally dispossessed, cut off, from the process of their genesis. However, by the same movement, we are also surreptitiously delivered, as in the French history, Joan of Arc is said to have been delivered to the English, that is, hand and foot tied. The object has become what its etymology suggests: what is thrown in front of (us), that is to say no longer as a scout for human adventure, but as the obstacle that prevents us from moving forward.

Because we only encounter things, tools or machines which have been prepared for a determined future, that is to say for the use for which they are intended, and which are therefore prisoners of this intended use, whether it is explicit or, more slyly, implicit and hidden. But this intended use can obviously be nothing other than a repetition, and even a repetition of repetitions. So that in the use, that is to say is in the *future* of the object, we find again the same repetitive serial production process that brought the object into existence and which constituted its past before it became this kind of *amnesia* that builds up any merchandise as such.

It's hard to imagine a more insidious and effective way of spreading a conformism of such a nearly dizzying accuracy. Objects do exactly what they were designed to do and, by consequence, when they use them, humans act in the way that was planned and designed for them. It is no longer the Devil who hides in the details, but on the contrary, a particularly insidious and unconscious kind of Police. If some computer scientists have said about interactive software "code is the law", they only revealed a much older state of affairs which is the fact that each object makes Police and Justice, The Law and the Prophets. Any man-machine, man-tool, man-object interface is designed to determine how the object or machine will be used. That is to say, it determines even our gestures. And there is no evidence that it does it with any kind of benevolence, but neither the designers nor the users seem to care. As for the employers of designers, we know that their main concern is that these interfaces serve their financial interests. And these are a variety of memes that Richard Dawkins seems to have forgotten to talk about.

Moreover, the principle of serial mass production

of identical objects, obviously consists in excluding any accident. Particularly this accidental part that creeps in, like it or not, in any artisanal production. But it should also be noted that any accident is just as well excluded from the use, which, in practice, is hardly less repetitive than what occurs in serial production. This somewhat depressing situation is usually masked by declaring that use is strictly individual and that it belongs to the realm of privacy. So that we live in a highly individualistic world in which everything is serial mass-produced, and in which everyone therefore necessarily does exactly the same as everyone else, but supposedly in secret. We can try to believe it, and even against all odds to some extent we succeed believing it. This does not prevent the fact that nothing kills love inspiration like hearing the neighbors on Saturday evening engage in the same kind of merry practices as yourself, at around the same time and 30 centimeters from you, on the other side of the wall ... Thus, on one side, the past of the object has gone by the wayside and on the other, the future of the object has disappeared in the "mysterious" depths of intimacy. No wonder that we live in an eternal present, in this eternal glory of the merchandise that sits in its shop window.

This loss of contact with the Real is not only individual, but it is also, and much more deeply, *collective*. In free collective work, contact with the real world is offered to the actors of a jointly implemented production process that is created, executed and controlled by the actors themselves. This collective production process necessarily requires and creates a language. But when men are collectively dispossessed of all contact with the technical world as well as with the supposedly non-technical world of the use, when work, and life outside work, no longer allow us this contact with the world, the poetic capacities of language drastically shrink, or rather collapse.

And this is certainly what Annie Le Brun noted in *Du trop de réalité* and even more clearly in *Appel d'Air* without really achieving to name and identify - as far as I could perceive, at least - the root causes of this silent disappearance of the poetic capacities of everyday language.

Words lose their meaning and their resonances because everyday technical life itself loses its meaning. Or rather for the simple reason that it disappears. Words lose their meaning because *meaning is attached to action*, because meaning is a revelation, because meaning is revealed by the uncertainties in which all action occurs. While each profession had created its own language, its own slang - actual slang being only the special case of the professional language of thieves, murderers and crooks - when the trades and crafts themselves disappear, and their particular languages with them, then common language is cut off from a considerable source of expressions, words and even new syntactic possibilities, to say nothing of the associated semantic collapse.

The languages of trades and crafts are intimately penetrated by action. They are always heavily loaded with meaning because any action involves risks and therefore systematically requires a minimum of care and caution. Trades and crafts almost always incorporate dialect traits, traces of the areas where a given activity was born or reached its highest level. They often make extensive use of metaphors, sexual or not, but even the smallest thesaurus of these professional languages would easily reveal their poetic load. As is the case too with the popular names of many species of plants.

When the languages of the crafts and trades – that is to say the languages of human work – are lost, then language is reduced to this language of managers of various hierarchical levels, whose essential function is to *lie*. Managers must lie to their superiors to let them know that everything is going for the best, but they must also lie to their subordinates to encourage them to work more and better, in order to increase profits of which they will hardly or never benefit. And, even more often, in order to convince their subordinates that the new organization of work, recently and brilliantly conceived by people who never worked, constitutes a noticeable improvement or a promising step forward.

Managers' activities essentially consists of doing nothing, creating nothing, producing nothing, but simply transmitting towards lower levels, orders intended for the real producers, recording the results and reporting towards higher levels on the correct execution of orders and on the excellence of the results reached. The art of managers excels in the use spreadsheets software (and the associated highly original little drawings) and in producing presentation "slides", as elegant as they are concise, which their superiors demand that they summarize the totality of the reality and human thought in less than 5 slides. Two "tools" whose modernity is now so firmly established that there is every reason to believe it eternal.

It goes without saying that language itself then has no other possibility left than to become more and more abstract, more and more "formal", as Bounoure and Effenberger already noted in 1976 in La Civilization Surréaliste regarding the Postwar Structuralist fashion. Language is no longer even the support of lies, but much more exactly that of emptiness, of pure nothingness. And the type of poetry associated with this type of language is the very subtle art of saying nothing, while letting the interlocutors believe that something has been said. In other words, the lie has now deployed within the very act of speaking. Obviously, we can no longer speak of language at all, but of simulacrum.

Such is the current state of language. And the same obviously stands, if not worse, as regards images, which now aim primarily to connect us to the fundamental void of money, as illustrated in *Ce qui n'a pas de prix*, Annie Le Brun's recent (although somewhat late) book.

However, on the reverse side of such a situation, if the field of surrealist investigation and action were extended to encompass the unconscious powers that allow human beings to learn, we could renew the contact that our mind and our bodies are constantly building with the world itself. A world that we only know through this permanent creative activity of the mind and body. In other words, we would then reconnect with the very sources of poetry.

If the above analysis contains some truth, then it

implies reconnecting ourselves with *work*. And I fear my reader will stop reading this text at this very point. Of course I do not mean reconnecting with salaried work, but with the collective and free production of the totality of what constitutes human lives. In other words, *a common art of doing, of living and of knowing.*

In the surrounding mental confusion, everyone persists, through feigned negligence, to use the word "work" for what is in fact almost always nothing else than being an employee. The difference is however fundamental ... Work transforms the world, while being an employee on the contrary perpetuates the state of things. Assimilating work to employment is therefore to say that there is nothing else to do in this world than to perpetuate what is there. Everyone can see the excellence of the semantic maneuver : a garanteed castrating effect, equivalent to the famous "There Is No Alternative" of the regrettable Margaret Thatcher.

In the ordinary Novlang , "transforming the world" in Marx's sense can simply no longer be enunciated. One can no longer hope anything but being an employee in this world, that is to say, for example with regard to the French newspaper of the same name (« Le Monde »), to participate in interpreting it. Some readers may still recall that in times now immemorial, in Physics, the word "Work" was a strict equivalent of the word "Energy". Energy – of which it must be recalled that it cannot be created nor destroyed, and even much less saved – however still constitutes in Physics the inextricable correlate of any transformation. Yet an employee does not transform anything at all. It collects, records, synthesizes, produces various kinds of accounting reports, in short, an employee manages the world... Being an employee, in the end, always smacks of Kafka, that is to say, of the emptiness and bureaucratic absurdity, computerized or not.

It is vaguely felt that the joint generalization of the employee's condition and of the dissemination of any form of effective work to the antipodes of the planet must not be for nothing in the immense loss of any will to live that is a characteristic of the current time.

While the revolutionaries of the 1960s and 1970s could still speak of "the will to live" – despite the shadow cast by some doubts even in this time – to speak of a "will to live" in the "developed countries" of the 21st century is now to risk trigger some hints of hilarity - and maybe even more than hints. Let's call it today's form of black humor.

The current *anesthesia* has reached such depths, that the citizen of "democratic countries" can hardly be awakened by any means, would it be by the explosion of a bomb on his threshold or by the cannon of a Kalashnikov pointed at him when opening his front door...

It is not trivial to recall that men do not live only on bread, but also, and even much more radically, on poetry. The trouble is, that poetry has quite concretely almost disappeared, together with free collective work, as I suggested above. And consequently the desire to live, which only held by this thin thread of poetry, disappeared with it. This is the reason for this vertiginous anesthesia by which what has all the exterior of an irremediable addiction to capitalism is currently maintained. Everything indicates that everyone prefers - and by far - to die by Capital than to venture to live.

The current ecological crisis now shows that, in the relatively short term, the alternative is, either die under the boots of mafias of all kinds, or resolve to freely and collectively produce the totality of human life. Which was once called « work ». Which quite simply means setting up and developing cooperatives and cooperative networks, here and now.

The old workers' movement continues to think and act as if the people were still totally deprived of any means to produce. But these means, capitalism itself sold them to us. They are everywhere - asleep in closets, basements, attics, garages and workshops. You don't even need to change the private property rules of these production means, you just need to change the practices, pool them and use them collectively. Of course, the quality of these tools, usually built in the pitiful People's Republic of China, does not really make them sustainable, but still, they are enough to learn, to collectively learn and progress.

Without a long and progressive habituation to free collective work, without the practical resolution of the problems associated with it, one can be assured that each "Grand Soir" will only lead to establishing a new mafia, whether of the "Soviet" type or another. Because the problems posed by the establishment of free work communities are not necessarily simple, and they will certainly not be solved by the magic of any revolutionary "Grand

Soir" whatsoever.

That's all ! I attempted here to point out some means suitable to recover both freedom and poetry, and this, maybe, to a degree deeper than was ever been suggested. The ongoing ecological crisis and the likely collapse of the current civilization will obviously force us to move in these directions. Yet, the game is both risky and subtle, and the appalling absence of any will to live currently makes success rather unlikely.

For the time being, I must admit that such a project has almost no chance of meeting the slightest adhesion in the still somewhat warm ashes of what once was the surrealist adventure. Surrealism is today reduced to the more or less unfortunate artistic, literary or poetic exploitation of a vein which had however originally opened up a field of thought and action of a much wider scope, and which was charged with much larger ambitions. Of course, I am aware of this situation, but I do not accept it.

Pierre Petiot - 2018-2021

Photo : Zazie

Possessions Ordinaires

Table des Matières

Introduction

Afin de suggérer l'étendue du domaine que les pages qui suivent tentent de baliser partiellement, il n'est peut-être pas inutile de faire état de la manière dont ces considérations me sont historiquement apparues, il y a désormais presque quarante ans, dans les années 1980-1985 ...

Je me souviens fort bien avoir alors écrit à une amie : « *Les idées nous **possèdent**, en un sens presque vaudou du terme* ». Il ne s'agissait pas alors pour moi de désigner par là un champ de nature instrumentale ou technique comme je vais le faire dans les pages qui suivent, mais bien d'une remarque beaucoup plus générale et d'ailleurs initialement essentiellement relative au domaine plus proprement intellectuel...

Quelques années plus tard, Richard Dawkins développait sa théorie des *memes*. [Cf. Dawkins, Richard (1989), "*11. Memes: the new replicators*", *The Selfish Gene* (2nd ed., new ed.), Oxford: Oxford University Press, p. 368, ISBN 0-19-217773-7], bien que l'idée comme le terme de *memes* aient une origine plus ancienne dans sa pensée.

L'une de mes préoccupations à l'époque était de trouver un sens plausible au concept assez vague de *Grands Transparents* tel qu'évoqué par André Breton, et il me semblait que les idées et systèmes d'idées, qui tels des virus invisibles et abstraits, « parasitent » les cerveaux humains et par leur intermédiaire, se propagent à travers des groupes humains importants et même des civilisations entières, sans considération aucune des intérêts de l'espèce, pouvaient fournir un bon exemple de *Grands Transparents*.

L'idée est assez proche de celle des mèmes de Richard Dawkins, mais elle est en même temps différente, car l'image de base qui sous-tend mon point de vue n'est pas de nature biologique, mais plutôt, faute de mieux, « supra biologique », ou « émergente » par rapport à la biologie, au sens où la culture *émerge* de la nature. Mais elle est aussi d'une portée plus générale que l'idée des mèmes, puisqu'elle prend en compte le fait que nous ne pouvons absolument pas penser – ni même d'ailleurs humainement exister – sans images, ni sans idées.

Que nous devions, certes, nous méfier des images et des idées, parce qu'elles ne sont pas « nous » et vivent une vie indépendante, la crise écologique actuelle le démontre assez, qui résulte de conceptions issues des pratiques inaugurées au Néolithique d'une part, et d'autre part de leurs héritières en l'espèce du système de pensées et de pratiques capitalistes. Mais nous devons nécessairement *vivre avec*, les images et les idées parce que d'une certaine manière elles sont « nous » *aussi*. Il me semble que la vision de Richard Dawkins est plus proche de celle de virus parasitant l'humanité, tandis que celle que je propose est plus proche de l'idée d'une *symbiose* obligatoire. Une symbiose sans laquelle, ni les images, ni les idées, ni les modèles, ni par dessus tout l'espèce humaine elle-même ne peuvent survivre.

Quant aux Grands Transparents, j'ai appris depuis lors, et en fait assez récemment, dans « *Entretiens Morphologiques, Notebook N°1 1936-1944* » publié par Germana Ferrari aux Editions Sistan Limited en 1987, que l'idée des Grands Transparents avait été inventée par Matta avant d'être reprise par Breton. C'était l'époque où Breton songeait à un Troisième Manifeste du Surréalisme, et ce qui était visé, dit Matta, ce n'était rien de moins que le passage d'un surréalisme littéraire à un surréalisme conceptuel. Matta note à ce sujet que Breton a donné à cette idée un contenu assez différent de celui que lui-même avait en tête en la proposant à Breton. Matta dit que Breton a limité les Grands Transparents en les rendant « anthropomorphes ».

La représentation que Breton se fait des Grands Transparents, est celle d'êtres d'une nature et d'une dimension (ou éventuellement d'un nombre de dimensions) radicalement au-delà de la compréhension humaine, tout comme les fourmis ne peuvent concevoir ce que sont les êtres humains. La conception de Matta est très différente... Ce que lui identifie comme un exemple de Grands Transparents, c'est plutôt le système de communication des fourmis, système qui modèle leurs interactions et donne forme et conditionne l'existence même de la fourmillière, et donc l'existence des fourmis comme espèce elle-même.

Il donne d'autres exemples à titre indicatif comme le système des ondes hertziennes, ou la conformation dynamique des vents dans les cyclones. Autrement dit, la vision de Matta s'enracine dans des représentations d'origine scientifique (et tente de les dépasser) tandis que celle de Breton, pour qui la notion de mythe est une préoccupation centrale à l'époque, reste plutôt d'ordre « mythologique ».

Dans le chapitre qui va suivre, j'ai choisi d'utiliser largement le langage de la « possession ». Non pas certes pour des raisons religieuses, ni folkloriques, ni liées en quoi que ce soit à ce qu'on appelle l'Occultisme, *au contraire*. L'objectif de ce texte est de faire sortir les phénomènes associés des domaines de l'ésotérisme et des religions et de montrer qu'il s'agit d'une caractéristique normale de l'esprit humain. Cependant, l'usage du vocabulaire de la possession me permet de tenter une généalogie, une génèse de la manière dont le cerveau humain fonctionne, disons depuis... « La nuit des temps » et la manière dont il a évolué.

Il me semble que le fonctionnement de base de l'esprit humain doit être resté sensiblement le même depuis l'apparition de Sapiens, et il ne semble d'ailleurs pas avoir subi de modifications biologiques notables. De sorte que ce qui fait la différence entre la pensée des chasseurs-cueilleurs et la nôtre, ce sont les artefacts (images, idées, outils) que nous avons créé au fil de l'histoire de l'espèce. Des artefacts que nous hantons tout autant qu'ils nous hantent.

Dans ce qui va suivre, il pourra aussi sembler que je me restreigne à la dimension « technique » des choses. Mais on aurait cependant tort d'en rester à cet avis parce que d'une part, il ne s'agit que d'un exemple, et d'autre part, parce que du point de vue dont ces pages sont écrites, il n'y a pas de différence essentielle entre les différents types d'artefacts avec lesquels et grâce auxquels nous vivons, qu'il s'agisse d'images, d'idées, d'outils, ou même de modèles scientifiques, et il ne me semble donc pas judicieux de discriminer entre des choses dites abstraites (images, d'idées, modèles) et des choses dites concrètes (outils, machines, mise en œuvre de procédures techniques, et technologies).

Les lecteurs que la terminologie de « possession » gènerait pourront la remplacer par « simulation mentale » car à moins de croire pour de bon aux « esprits », il ne me semble pas qu'il y ait lieu de faire la différence. L'expérience du shaman ne me semble en fait différer de l'expérience humaine ordinaire que par le choix *conscient* et *délibéré* de la mise en œuvre d'une exploration mentale particulièrement *intense* du monde.

Danse de l'esprit et des choses

D'une manière peut-être pas si éloignée de cette écriture gestuelle automatique sur quoi se fonde le Butô dans un élan fait autant de passion que d'abandon, en termes d'imagination de la matière, il y avait toujours eu la barbe de Gaston Bachelard sur mon épaule. Mais plus récemment, un ami, par une heureuse inadvertance, m'a désigné l'oeuvre de Malcolm de Chazal...

« Puisque l'eau est totalement détendue et que, dans le même courant, aucun de ses gestes n'est contraint et empesé, puisque l'eau est la simplicité absolue, l'aisance même, et puisqu'on ne peut simplifier ce qui est déjà l'essence du simple, pour "découvrir" l'eau donc, il nous faut trouver autre chose. Et cette autre chose -- cette condition essentielle -- c'est *d'ajouter* à l'eau, comme on ajoute à une substance une autre substance pour provoquer une réaction et la "révéler". Et ce réactif qu'on ajoute à l'eau pour la découvrir, c'est *soi-même* qu'on intègre à l'âme de l'eau, de la façon suivante. L'homme qui voit couler un cours d'eau oubliera après un certain temps qu'il est lui, et se sentira peu à peu "devenir" l'eau qui coule – faisant siens les gestes de l'eau elle-même, comme l'amoureux s'abolit dans le visage aimé et pense et agit les moindre gestes de son visage jusqu'à ce sentir disparu au sein de la vie d'un autre, englouti et comme fondu dans sa substance. Cette intégration, qui est tout le contraire du narcissisme, nous fera bientôt "penser eau", "agir eau", "vivre eau", nous mettant forcément peu à peu dans un autre vase de connaissance, sur un autre plan de vie, sur un autre degré de conscience... »

Malcolm de Chazal - *La Vie Filtrée* Pages 88-89 - Collection Imaginaire Gallimard - Gallimard 1949

Dans cette page de Malcolm de Chazal, il y a plus que du Surréalisme. Il y a un lien profond avec le Butô et les expériences de possession qui font partie du Butô, sans pour autant vraiment faire partie du Surréalisme, lequel n'aborde le plus souvent la possession que de l'extérieur. Le texte de Malcolm de Chazal peut être également relié aux mythes et aux chansons associées dans lesquels deux sorciers rivalisent de magie et d'imagination en se transformant successivement en animaux, plantes ou en d'autres choses et êtres différents. Non seulement on peut trouver chez Malcolm de Chazal certains aspects des phénomènes de possession qui sont à la source du Butô, mais il se trouve que dans le texte de De Chazal, ils sont également liés à la danse ...

« Tous les gestes de la nature se résument en un mouvement de danse. [...] Ainsi, tout mouvement imprimé à l'eau fait s'animer tout d'abord la *danse première* comme un tout -- danse première existant déjà en principe-essence dans l'eau, étant le point de départ même de la forme de l'Informé. Aussi le mouvement de danse dans l'eau est-il double : la *danse première* qui, dans l'Informé, lui a imprimé une forme-essence, et la *danse secondaire* qui, telle une enveloppe de danse

autour d'un noyau-danse, fait danser l'eau
comme un tout et fait redanser en lui-même le
"coeur de danse" de l'eau, qui est son
mouvement pivotal et initial, sa danse
primaire... »

Malcolm de Chazal - *La Vie Filtrée* P72-73 - Collection
Imaginaire Gallimard - Gallimard 1949

Mais on sait aussi que ce lien entre danse et
possession n'est nullement restreint au Butô ni à la
perception de De Chazal, mais très largement
répandu parmi les peuples qui n'ont pas été
contaminés par les religions abrahamiques.

Pourtant, le Butô semble en réalité masquer
quelque chose que Malcolm de Chazal souligne à
juste titre. Et c'est que la possession n'est pas un
état d'exception qui serait lié aux mouvements
toujours un peu spectaculaires de la transe. C'est
en fait l'état normal de Malcolm de Chazal au
moment même où il écrit. Et c'est aussi le nôtre
lorsque nous le lisons – dans la mesure, bien sûr,
où nous acceptons de partager son état d'esprit
pour comprendre ce qu'il veut dire.

Pourtant, nous avons tous vécu consciemment de
tels états de possession lorsque nous étions
enfants. Nous connaissions alors tous ce *"faire
comme si"* dans toute sa profondeur et son
intensité :

« L'enfant apprend beaucoup plus par son jouet
que par mille formes de conversations – son
jouet : ce premier des points de départ de sa
pensée, lieu où il commença en premier à
inimager, puis à *imaginer*, car par cette

limitation de son champ visuel que crée
l'instinct possessif, l'enfant se cloître par son
jouet à un champ restreint de pensée, et, ne
pouvant transporter d'autre images dans ce
bibelot limité, l'enfant est forcé d'y mettre du
sien et *d'imager* en plein centre de lui-même, de
se "transplanter" dans son jouet, de faire des
constructions de son propre esprit et de son
propre moi dans cette piste fermée de la vie,
terrain subitement muré contre les images du
dehors ».

Malcolm de Chazal - *La Vie Filtrée* P58 - Collection
Imaginaire Gallimard - Gallimard 1949

Si Malcolm de Chazal pointe à juste titre un
phénomène important, un phénomène d'une
importance critique, même, en ce qu'il éclaire la
façon dont nos esprits se construisent,
progressivement, certains aspects de son
interprétation me semblent discutables...

Le premier est le rôle ou la fonction de ce qu'il
appelle « l'instinct possessif » de l'enfant dans
l'ensemble du processus. Il devrait en fait savoir
mieux et davantage que ce qu'il en dit ici, puisque
dans les citations ci-dessus à propos de l'eau, il
indique clairement, en laissant de côté le
narcissisme, que l'esprit humain, lorsqu'il est
possédé par l'esprit de l'eau, n'est évidemment
plus du tout hanté par lui-même, et encore moins
par une sorte d'instinct possessif. Mais plutôt tout
le contraire.

Le deuxième problème que soulève l'interprétation
de De Chazal, je crois, c'est le besoin qu'aurait
spécifiquement l'enfant de plonger dans « un sol

soudainement muré contre les images de l'extérieur ». Si l'enfant doit faire cela ce n'est pas parce qu'il est un enfant, mais tout simplement parce qu'il est un être humain. Dans la mesure où nous souhaitons investir un objet ou un être donné au moyen de notre esprit, à partir de l'intérieur de nous-mêmes, quel que soit notre âge, nous devons tous nous déposséder de l'emprise du monde extérieur pour nous laisser posséder, envahir, par l'objet ou l'être en question. C'est d'ailleurs très clair également dans la citation précédente où De Chazal nous parle de l'eau.

Le troisième problème que me semble poser la formulation de De Chazal est : quel est le but de ce jeu de possession mentale que les enfants jouent en eux-mêmes lorsqu'ils sont laissés seuls et même lorsqu'ils jouent avec d'autres enfants ? Il s'agit d'une activité si typique et si fréquente qu'elle doit probablement remplir une fonction biologique importante, ou importante au moins du point de vue de la biologie humaine. De Chazal voit et dit bien que l'enfant « apprend beaucoup plus par son jouet que par mille autre formes de conversation », mais il reste silencieux sur ce point décisif : Qu'est-ce que les enfants apprennent réellement de cette façon?

Ma réponse personnelle serait qu'ils n'apprennent rien de spécifique, sauf faire ce qu'ils font, c'est-à-dire se laisser posséder par les choses qui les entourent, afin de saisir mentalement ces choses et de devenir capables *d'anticiper*, de *deviner* le comportement de ces choses ou de ces êtres. Tandis que les objets choisis pour exercer ce genre de compétence n'ont aucune importance - "juste des jouets" - le processus lui-même est probablement d'une importance critique...

Antiquité de pratiques modernes

Il y a quelques années, un documentaire télévisé montrait des chasseurs-cueilleurs traquant des animaux. Tandis que certains d'entre eux, superstitieux, tentaient d'obtenir les bonnes grâces des esprits de la chasse locaux au moyen de pratiques magiques, d'autres n'en faisaient rien. Mais tous utilisaient leurs capacités à se laisser posséder par l'esprit des animaux qu'ils chassaient, afin de deviner où allaient leurs proies et où elles se cachaient.

Si de telles capacités ont été essentielles à la survie de l'humanité pendant des centaines de milliers d'années, on peut être assuré qu'elles le sont toujours dans notre vie quotidienne, d'une manière probablement évidente, bien que dissimulée.

On peut rendre les choses plus sensibles sur la base d'une histoire dont j'ai été témoin dans le domaine même de la logique : le développement de logiciels.

Il y a environ 15 ou 20 ans, les responsables des activités de développement logiciel d'IBM ont décidé de réagir face au nombre important, désagréable, potentiellement dangereux et surtout très coûteux, d'erreurs résiduelles laissées dans les logiciels. Après quelques enquêtes, ils ont fini par trouver un moyen efficace de supprimer les erreurs des logiciels nouvellement développés en mettant en place ce qu'ils ont appelé un système « d'inspection ».

Le procédé consistait à faire relire le code de leur logiciel par plusieurs programmeurs afin d'identifier les problèmes et les erreurs. En enregistrant le nombre d'erreurs trouvées par millier de lignes de code et en réalisant des statistiques basées sur ces données enregistrées, ils ont prouvé que ces pratiques d'inspection étaient beaucoup plus efficaces en termes de détection et suppression d'erreurs que les tests traditionnels du logiciel eux-mêmes.

Comme le mot "inspection" sonnait de manière assez désagréable aux oreilles des développeurs, ces pratiques ont ensuite été rebaptisées "Revues par les Pairs", une formulation plus courante dans le domaine de la recherche et de l'édition scientifiques.

L'entreprise pour laquelle je travaillais à ce moment-là a décidé de mettre en place le même type de processus de revues par les pairs, mais le nombre moyen de défauts détectés pour mille lignes de logiciel grâce aux revues par les pairs dans cette entreprise était bien en deçà des chiffres annoncés par IBM. Nous avons donc demandé à d'anciens ingénieurs d'IBM devenus consultants, d'étudier la raison pour laquelle nous avions de si piètres résultats.

Après quelques heures passées à étudier nos pratiques, les consultants américains nous ont finalement dit que nous devions énoncer mentalement, ou même à haute voix, le texte de nos logiciels et l'interpréter un peu comme dans une pièce de théâtre, faute quoi l'efficacité de notre processus de détection de défauts au moyen de revues par les pairs resterait faible et et nos efforts presque inutiles. Comme je savais déjà à ce moment-là comment procédaient les chasseurs dans les groupes de chasseurs-cueilleurs lorsqu'ils traquaient leurs proies, ma conclusion personnelle (restée secrète) fut que nous devions atteindre le point où nous nous sentirions, dans une certaine mesure, habités, possédés, par notre code logiciel.

Tout développeur de logiciels, et de même tout ingénieur dans la conception de systèmes complexes, sait bien que, lorsqu'il se trouve bloqué par un problème ou un bogue, le meilleur moyen de sortir de l'impasse consiste à décrire le problème à haute voix devant un ami ou un collègue, tout en faisant si possible nombre de diagrammes sur un tableau noir. En fait, le collègue que vous avez choisi pour cela n'a nullement besoin d'écouter ce que vous dites ni de regarder vos diagrammes. A vrai dire, cela s'avère même tout à fait inutile. Pourtant, généralement, au bout de moins d'une demi-heure de gestes véhéments effectués devant le vide total d'attention que vous oppose votre très indifférent collègue, vous trouvez généralement la solution à un problème qui vous préoccupait pourtant depuis une ou deux semaines. Ceci simplement parce que que votre ami, qui ne s'occupait pourtant que de ses affaires en attendant que vous ayez fini votre petite scène de théâtre, vous a gentiment servi d'audience virtuelle. Telles sont la puissance et la sagesse de la possession...

Généralité des simulations mentales

Bien avant l'introduction des revues par les pairs, dans les équipes de développement logiciel, chaque développeur savait intuitivement qu'interpréter mentalement le texte de ses programmes constituait une condition préalable pour qu'il puisse espérer que ces programmes fonctionnent correctement. C'est la raison pour laquelle il n'est pas si rare d'entendre un développeur de logiciels parler à haute voix lorsqu'il travaille dans un endroit où il se sait – ou se croit – seul.

Et si vous avez développé une oreille attentive à cet type de phénomène et qu'il vous arrive d'observer quelques techniciens au travail, vous vous rendrez vite compte que n'importe lequel d'entre eux, lorsqu'il est confronté à un problème technique un peu difficile, essaie de se tirer d'affaire en tentant de caractériser en lui-même, à voix basse ou même à haute voix, le problème qui lui résiste. Encore n'ai-je rien dit des gestes qui accompagnent souvent ce mode d'expression spontané dès lors qu'un peu de géométrie dans l'espace vient se mêler aux difficultés rencontrées.

Instruit par Malcolm de Chazal, je dirais qu'en pareille situation, les gens tentent de *laisser entrer le problème en eux-mêmes* – autre formulation du même phénomène spontané de *possession volontaire*.

On retrouvera des conduites similaires en observant une personne qui essaie de se convaincre de la validité d'une preuve mathématique non triviale. Ceci, bien que les mathématiques soient (un peu rapidement, d'ailleurs) généralement considérées comme le domaine par excellence de la rationalité consciente d'elle-même.

Encore plus couramment, « apprendre quelque chose par cœur » implique les mêmes mécanismes et, exprimer et répéter en nous-mêmes les choses dont nous voulons nous souvenir, que ce soit à haute voix ou en silence est généralement requis d'une manière ou d'une autre.

Sur la base d'observations aussi générales, on peut penser que de tels phénomènes se produisent (bien que de manière silencieuse voire inconsciente) chaque fois qu'un être humain est confronté à l'utilisation d'un outil, d'une machine ou plus généralement lorsqu'il est confronté à une tâche "matérielle" ou "intellectuelle" qui n'est pas encore devenue un automatisme. En tant qu'êtres humains, il semble que la seule approche dont nous disposions pour anticiper ce qui peut arriver lorsque nous utilisons un objet technique (et toutes les choses qui nous entourent sont des objets techniques, y compris une bonne partie des chemins balisés qu'empruntent nos pensées) est – pour ainsi dire – de laisser "l'esprit" de cet objet technique entrer en nous, ou « d'entrer mentalement » nous-mêmes dans cet objet technique. Dès lors, puisque notre environnement humain quotidien est principalement constitué d'objets techniques – fourchettes, couteaux et cuillères même – cela signifie que cette sorte de "théâtre de possession" conscient ou beaucoup plus souvent inconscient est toujours actif quelque part dans notre cerveau. En d'autres termes, nous « simulons » intérieurement notre environnement (technique ou non d'ailleurs) en permanence.

Pourtant, il convient de restreindre la portée de l'hypothèse qui vient d'être énoncée parce qu'elle ne s'applique que pour des tâches qui ne sont pas encore devenues des automatismes. On sait en effet qu'une fois qu'un comportement est devenu un automatisme, il migre vers ce qu'il est convenu d'appeler la *mémoire procédurale*, qui est un type de mémoire inconsciente au sens ou nous n'avons plus besoin de faire appel à notre petit « théâtre de possession » pour marcher, parler, nager ou faire du vélo, toutes choses dont l'apprentissage avait pourtant originellement requis une dose importante *d'attention*.

Mémoire procédurale

Si toute mise en œuvre tant soit peu complexe d'objets technique au cours de notre vie quotidienne implique toujours une composante de simulation préalable destinée à nous permetre de prévoir le résultat de nos actes et le comportement de l'objet, cette étape de simulation peut être consciente ou inconsciente, ou même apparemment absente lorsqu'il s'agit d'actions qui sont presque devenues de l'ordre du réflexe. Mais on peut songer que de manière générale, il n'existe pas de frontière nette entre conscient et inconscient en matière procédurale ou technique.

Quant à l'inconscient procédural, la situation est très différente de ce qui a cours dans le domaine de l'inconscient freudien où le refoulement empêche certains éléments inconscients de parvenir à la conscience. Bien entendu les mêmes phénomènes de refoulements peuvent intervenir aussi dans le domaine de l'inconscient procédural lorsque des évévements traumatiques se trouvent historiquement intiment liés à un apprentissage ou à la mise en œuvre de certaines procédures de nature technique.

Mais il est facile de comprendre pourquoi il *doit* y avoir continuité ou gradation entre conscient et inconscient techniques. En effet, bien qu'une grande partie de nos gestes soient exécutés de manière automatique (comme marcher, ou appuyer sur un interrupteur pour allumer la lumière par exemple etc.), dès que les choses se complexifient ou bien ne se passent pas comme prévu, notre *attention* doit prendre le relais.

Et il me semble préférable de parler ici *d'attention* plutôt que de *conscience* car pour des raisons dont l'origine religieuse ou au mieux philosophique ne fait guère de doute, on a fait trop de cas de la conscience, que l'on se représente comme une caractéristique spécifiquement humaine, dont les animaux seraient totalement ou presque totalement dépourvus. L'emploi du terme *attention* permet en revanche de prendre en compte le fait que les capacités d'attention de beaucoup d'animaux peuvent être aisément observées, même par les philosophes idéalistes et les religieux les plus endurcis, et que leur existence ne laisse guère place au doute. Considérer par exemple que l'attention d'un prédateur à l'affût puisse ne pas être fortement mobilisée, serait en effet faire preuve d'un genre de mauvause foi difficilement acceptable.

Neurones miroirs

Pendant longtemps, les phénomènes de possession ont été le plus souvent associés à la transe ou aux effets des drogues qui l'accompagnent souvent. Pour spectaculaires que soient ces choses là, Malcolm de Chazal est sans doute plus proche de la vérité lorsqu'il insiste sur ce qu'il appelle *l'Imitation instinctive*, qu'il identifie à ce qu'il appelle aussi le « *dédoublement* ». D'ailleurs, peut-être le mot « dédoublement » est-il au fond plus précis et adéquat que le mot « possession » car une personne possédée ne cesse pas nécessairement d'être elle-même, elle n'est souvent possédée qu'en partie, ou bien possédée seulement par intermittence.

> « L'imitation instinctive. [...] Par cette loi d'*imitation instinctive*, tel homme, par exemple, imitera inconsciemment tel autre individu avec lequel il vit en communauté, quelque puissante pourrait être sa propre personnalité -- personnalité que l'autre en retour imitera avec d'autant plus de force que sera faible la sienne -- le plus fort ici se faisant toujours plus imiter qu'il n'imite, l'imitation allant dans le sens et dans les régions de moindre résistance de la personnalité et inscrivant son empreinte tout autant dans le physique que dans le moral ou dans le spirituel des gestes du corps aux mouvements de l'expression, de la mentalité à l'humeur, des goûts aux habitudes, imprimant son sceau à travers tout le champ des activités

et de la pensée de l'homme. Sans cette *loi d'imitation instinctive*, il n'y aurait point de société, de patrie, de nation, car l'individualité, déjà assez pressée par l'intérêt, déborderait partout et engloutirait tout. *L'imitation instinctive* est la force de cohésion des sociétés humaines. »

Malcolm de Chazal, Ibidem P117

Comme dans toutes les comparaisons entre fort et faible, meilleur ou pire, adapté ou non adapté, etc. il faut se poser la question du contexte et de l'échelle utilisée. Et Malcolm de Chazal ne fournit aucune précision sur ce point ici. La « force » d'une rose réside-t-elle dans son parfum, ses couleurs, sa résistance à la sécheresse ou aux changements de température, ou encore dans la durée de sa floraison ? Poser la question, c'est y répondre : tout dépend du contexte considéré et des points de vue.

Je laisserai donc ce mode de pensée relatif pour me concentrer sur ce qui l'est moins, à savoir le genre d'imitation instinctive dont parle ici De Chazal. Bien que les observations de cette nature soient relativement faciles, courantes et que nombre de gens les aient faites longtemps avant celles que rapporte De Chazal, nous savons maintenant qu'il ne s'agit plus simplement d'intuitions exigeant un degré de sensibilité et de subtilité auquel De Chazal nous a habitués, mais que c'est désormais de la science et une science que De Chazal ne pouvait connaître à l'époque où il écrivait La Vie Filtrée (1949), puisque les neurones miroirs n'ont été découverts que dans les années 1990 par

Giacomo Rizzolatti.

Voici, à tire indicatif, ce que l'on trouve à ce sujet dans la version française de Wikipedia...

> Les neurones miroirs sont une catégorie de neurones du cerveau qui présentent une activité aussi bien lorsqu'un individu exécute une action que lorsqu'il observe un autre individu (en particulier de son espèce) exécuter la même action, ou même lorsqu'il imagine une telle action, d'où le terme miroir. Ils sont connus pour être à l'origine du bâillement. Il existe également des neurones échos.
>
> En neurosciences cognitives, les neurones miroirs joueraient un rôle dans la cognition sociale, notamment dans l'apprentissage par imitation, mais aussi dans les processus affectifs, tels que l'empathie. Le professeur Ramachandran les appelle neurones empathiques.
>
> Les neurones miroirs sont considérés comme une découverte majeure en neurosciences. Si, pour certains chercheurs, ils constituent un élément central de la cognition sociale (depuis le langage jusqu'à l'art, en passant par les émotions et la compréhension d'autrui), pour d'autres, ces conclusions restent très hypothétiques quant au rôle de ces neurones dans ces processus psychologiques. Le rôle de ces neurones pour la cognition sociale humaine aurait ainsi été largement surévalué.

Il n'y a pas lieu ici de discuter en détails le rôle

exact des neurones miroirs dans la « cognition sociale » compte tenu du flou qui peut sembler entourer cette expression et de l'immense domaine qu'elle semble tenter de désigner... Il suffit de noter que l'existence des neurones miroirs fournissent un fondement biologique à ce que Malcolm De Chazal identifie sous le terme *d'imitation instinctive*. Quant au reste, les sciences de l'esprit ne sont nullement achevées et si l'existence de neurones miroirs suffisait à rendre compte de tous les aspects des cultures humaines, les chercheurs pourraient consacrer le reste de leurs jours à des vacances définitives.

Toujours à titre indicatif, car la fonction d'une encyclopédie en général ou de celle Wikipedia en particulier n'est pas de fournir au public un état des recherches les plus récentes, mais plus simplement d'éclairer le public pour lui permettre d'aller plus loin s'il le désire, poursuivons l'examen de l'article de Wikipedia...

> L'identification de neurones miroirs au cours des années 1990 est due à l'équipe de Giacomo Rizzolatti, directeur du département de neurosciences de la faculté de médecine de Parme.
>
> Ils ont d'abord été observés dans le cortex prémoteur ventral du singe macaque rhésus (aire F5) mais aussi, par la suite, dans la partie rostrale du lobule pariétal inférieur. Ce type de neurones a également été trouvé chez certains oiseaux où ils sont activés à la fois lors du chant et lorsque l'animal écoute un congénère chantant.

Chez l'humain, il existe depuis avril 2010 une preuve directe de l'existence de neurones miroirs. Jusqu'alors, étant donné les nombreuses homologies entre les cerveaux des différents primates, il était admis que de tels neurones devaient aussi exister chez l'espèce humaine. En outre, par imagerie cérébrale fonctionnelle (tomographie par émissions de positons ou imagerie par résonance magnétique fonctionnelle, par exemple), il est possible d'observer dans certaines régions du cortex cérébral (notamment autour de l'aire de Broca, homologue à l'aire F5 du singe, et au niveau du cortex pariétal inférieur) une activation à la fois quand l'individu produit une action et lorsqu'il observe un autre individu exécuter une action plus ou moins similaire. Mais, étant donné la résolution spatiale de ces techniques, rien ne permettait d'affirmer que ces activations provenaient exactement des mêmes neurones et non pas de deux populations de neurones entremêlée. Par précaution, on utilisait donc parfois les termes « système miroir » ou « système de neurones miroirs » plutôt que « neurones miroirs » pour désigner ces aires fonctionnelles.

Ce qui semble poser problème dans cette partie de l'article de wikipedia, c'est de déterminer la localisation précise des neurones miroirs. Ce point de vue « géographique » peut peut-être avoir un intérêt, mais on peut légitimement supposer que, comme beaucoup d'autres propriétés du cerveau, l'effet miroir n'est probablement pas une propriété de neurones pris isolément ni même une propriété d'assemblages particuliers de neurones, mais une propriété *émergente* de *réseaux* de neurones miroirs. Par propriété émergente, on entend ici une propriété qui n'a de sens et ne peut être correctement décrite qu'au niveau d'un réseau, et qui n'est pas déductible des propriétés individuelles des composants du réseaux eux-mêmes, en l'espèce, les neurones. Cette remarque peut paraître d'autant plus pertinente qu'il semble que, pour une part au moins, ce soient les mêmes neurones qui participent à la fois aux actions motrices réelles et aux actions motrices simulées provoquées par l'observation d'un congénère. Autrement dit, l'effet miroir consiste justement dans le fait l'activation des mêmes neurones au sein de réseaux différents peut conduire soit à des actions effectives, soit à des actions simulées et la question de savoir si un neurone ou un groupe de neurones est « miroir » ou non n'a pas grand sens.

Ce qui a du sens en revanche, c'est que ce que l'on sait des réseaux miroirs permet de comprendre que le terme de possession – qui n'est somme toute qu'une forme d'empathie excessive – n'est pas inapproprié, puisque les neurones miroirs constituent en réalité une véritable incarnation de l'activité et de « l'esprit » des autres en nous-mêmes. "Esprit" étant pris ici au sens strict de ce qui *anime* l'autre (mais âme - anima - dans son sens ancien et originel conviendrait peut-être mieux).

Le fait que l'imitation de l'autre ne se limite pas nécessairement aux membres d'une même espèce (animale ou humaine) est particulièrement perceptible chez nous en tant que primates,

puisqu'il est généralement admis que les singes...
Singent. Mais cela peut aussi s'observer par
intermittence chez nos espèces domestiques, par
exemple dans la propagation interspécifique du
baillement.

D'un autre côté, le fait que les animaux puissent
apprendre par imitation ne fait aucun doute. C'est
même l'une des façons dont ils apprennent le
mieux. Dans les procédés utilisés pour enseigner
de nouvelles connaissances aux perroquets, il était
d'usage de placer un maître (humain) devant un
perroquet (généralement un perroquet gris du
Gabon), le maître répétant sa leçon *devant* le
perroquet jusqu'à ce que le perroquet l'apprenne.
Cette méthode fonctionnait mais elle n'était pas
très efficace.

Les nouvelles procédures consistent désormais à
placer un autre animal (généralement un humain)
à côté du perroquet auquel on souhaite enseigner
quelque chose, le professeur (humain) enseignant
la même chose aux deux élèves, l'humain et le
perroquet. Avec cette nouvelle façon de faire, le
perroquet apprend par imitation, à la différence
toutefois que le perroquet n'imite plus le
professeur, mais l'élève humain et, lorsqu'il joue le
jeu avec une certaine passion, le perroquet
parvient parfois à donner la bonne réponse plus
rapidement que l'étudiant humain.

Mais Malcom de Chazal pousse un peu plus loin sa
conception de l'imitation instinctive et la
généralise à des contextes où les neurones miroirs
ne peuvent plus être remis en cause, car ils

n'existent pas, ou pas forcément.

«   Les règnes et les espèces sont les compléments les uns des autres -- les forces latentes des autres règnes et espèces poussant chaque unité particulière de la nature à imiter tant soit peu l'espèce avec laquelle elle vit en communauté et qu'elle coudoie ».

Malcolm de Chazal – Ibidem P118

Et De Chasal n'a pas tort dans la mesure où la nature ne manque pas de phénomènes de mimétisme   ;   d'animaux   imitant   leur environnement minéral (ex. Poulpes) ou végétal (ex. Phasmes) ou d'autres animaux (ex. animaux non dangereux imitant des animaux dangereux pour éloigner leurs prédateurs – ou mimétisme batésien), de plantes imitant des animaux (ex. Orchidées imitant le ventre d'un bourdon femelle pour attirer les bourdons mâles), de plantes imitant d'autres plantes (Passiflores imitant les feuilles d'autres plantes pour échapper aux mandibules des chenilles de leurs papillons prédateurs). Toutes ces mimétismes illustrent de manière frappante la propension du vivant, même inconscient, à imiter l'environnement minéral ou d'autres formes de vie.

Dans cette perspective, les neurones miroirs constituent en fait un cas particulier d'un ensemble de phénomènes «   d'imitation   » beaucoup plus généraux. Reste à élucider toutefois ce que veut réellement dire « imiter » au sens biologique, c'est à dire au-delà de l'usage ordinaire du mot.

Car il faut comprendre que ce qui est en jeu ici, ce n'est pas une variété de téléologie dans laquelle nous interpréterions un phénomène d'imitation naturel selon des critères intellectuels spécifiquement humains, en quelque sorte « tombés du Ciel », mais l'inverse. Ce sont nos critères intellectuels humains qui sont le résultat de l'évolution biologique et, dans le cas des réseaux miroirs – qui sont pour le moins l'une des bases de notre intellectualité –, d'une tendance de la vie à imiter qui, ayant fait ses preuves, a été sélectionnée à maintes reprises dans le cours de l'évolution, jusqu'à sa systématisation dans le cas particulier des réseaux neuronaux.

Cependant, Malcolm de Chazal centre généralement son discours sur l'aspect « psychique » de l'imitation instinctive chez l'homme, montrant que dans l'espèce humaine, l'imitation instinctive n'est nullement réduite aux domaines animal et intraspécifique humain...

> « Mais outre l'imitation des plantes par les animaux, il y a aussi l'imitation des plantes par l'homme. Mais ici l'imitation est moins directe. Elle est d'ordre psychique, participant de la faculté de dédoublement. Car en fait, ce qui fait croire à tant de narrateurs que la forêt s'anime, c'est qu'ils l'ont en eux, sensation qu'éprouve au plus haut point l'enfant, qui vierge encore du monde, est plus près de l'instinct que nous et s'intègre à la Nature. »

Malcolm de Chazal – Ibidem, P119

De manière générale nous avons tendance à faire

beaucoup trop de cas de l'intentionnalité. Les raisons de cette attitude s'enracinent évidemment dans les conceptions religieuses que dont nos civilisations ne parviennent toujours pas à s'extirper. Sans les notions de « faute » ou de « péché » qui se fondent sur l'intentionnalité, les religions perdraient largement leur influence. Mais aussi... les tribunaux et tout le système judiciaire qui se nourrissent également de la prétendue intentionnalité générale des actes humains. On dit que dans les peuples primitifs tout a une cause magique, et qu'il n'y a pas d'accidents, ni de morts accidentelles. Mais nous-mêmes faisons preuve à chaque instant d'un aveuglement comparable en ce que nous cherchons toujours obstinément des responsables à tout. Partout où l'intentionnalité magique était supposée rendre compte des événements humains, la magie a certes disparu, mais la référence à l'intentionnalité est restée.

Or, un siècle après Freud, l'intentionnalité n'est toujours pas questionnée. Il se sait confusément que *le moi n'est pas maître dans sa propre maison*, mais tout le monde continue de faire comme si c'était le cas. Qu'il puisse en être ainsi pour des raisons pratiques, passe encore. Mais les « sciences neuronales » elles-mêmes, semblent se donner pour objectif central l'élucidation de ce que pourrait bien être la *conscience*. Comme si la conscience était la chose la plus importante du monde... Comme si la conscience pouvait sortir toute armée du cerveau telle Minerve du crâne de Jupiter, ou nue comme la vérité sort du puits. Bien qu'il soit assez connu que « *rien n'a de sens en biologie si ce n'est à la lumière de l'évolution* », on persiste à étudier la conscience en soi, sans guère se préoccuper des circonstances évolutives qui ont pu en favoriser l'émergence. N'a-t-on pas pu lire dans un journal de vulgarisation scientifique que certains prétendaient avoir établi que la conscience reposait sur l'activité *d'un seul* neurone du cerveau et qu'ils savaient exactement lequel ! Dans l'état actuel des choses, on peut presque considérer que la définition la plus opérationnelle de la conscience, c'est de constituer, pour les journalistes et nombre chercheurs, l'un des meilleurs moyens de collecter des fonds.

Mais revenons à des considérations plus raisonnables. La question qui se pose est de savoir si cette i*mitation instinctive* dont parle De Chazal, par laquelle les êtres humains sont capables d'imiter, d'intérioriser ou peut-être plus précisément de *modéliser mentalement* presque tout, correspond sytématiquement à une activité des réseaux miroirs ou à celles d'autres types de réseaux de neurones.

Et ici, je préfère utiliser le terme de *modélisation* plutôt que les termes plus habituels d'imagination ou de représentation, car ces deux derniers termes ont une connotation plutôt statique, tandis que le terme de modélisation renvoie aux aspects dynamiques et comportementaux qui sont toujours intégrés dans les schémas mémoriels que notre cerveau élabore, réutilise et améliore constamment. Et il se peut bien que certains au moins des aspects dynamiques de la mémoire soient fournis par nos réseaux miroirs ou d'autres fonctionnements similaires.

La *modélisation* permet la *simulation*, et puisque notre cerveau n'importe pas pour de bon les objets réels dans notre tête, puisqu'il en enregistre la dynamique, et qu'il s'appuie sur elle pour agir, on peut dire que *notre cerveau simule.*

Pour autant, il serait inapproprié et surtout faux de dire d'un chaman qu'il simule, au sens plat qu'il prétendrait être l'esprit qui le possède. Il ne fait pas semblant. Il ne fait pas un show. Son but n'est pas d'impressionner le public. Non, *il essaie*. Il se met en mesure d'explorer l'inconnu

Tout comme un scientifique moderne exécute une simulation sur un ordinateur à partir d'un *modèle* qu'il a conçu, le chaman effectue lui aussi une simulation, à ceci près que l'ordinateur c'est lui-même et que ce que le chaman simule, c'est le *modèle* particulier de l'esprit dont il est possédé, ainsi que les interactions entre cet esprit extérieur et le sien. Et de même que le résultat d'une simulation informatique n'est pas connu à l'avance , sinon la simulation ne serait pas entreprise, le résultat de l'acte de possession volontaire auquel se prête le chaman est lourd de toutes les incertitudes de la vie. Car l'Esprit, comme on dit, *souffle où il veut*. Autre façon de dire comme l'a si bien signalé Mallarmé, que tout pensée émet un coup de dés.

Empreinte de l'outil

Il faut bien avouer qu'être hanté, habité par le monde comme j'espère avoir suggéré que nous le sommes, n'est probablement pas sans conséquences. Le monde humain est peuplé d'esprits, peuplé de choses et d'êtres vivants qui l'entourent, comme nous le démontrent les mythologies anciennes et lointaines, ainsi que les objets d'art et-ou rituels qui les hantaient. À une époque où les objets techniques étaient beaucoup plus rares et (bien que très sophistiqués) beaucoup moins complexes, les cerveaux humains étaient davantage peuplés d'objets naturels que ce n'est le cas aujourd'hui, de sorte qu'ils incorporaient principalement des êtres vivants, des animaux et des plantes, quelques lieux singuliers et... Bien sûr, déjà, beaucoup d'autres sortes d'esprits abstraits.

L'épuisement rapide des ressources écologiques locales utilisables que provoque le séjour quelque peu prolongé d'un groupe humain - même peu nombreux - a contraint les chasseurs-cueilleurs, non pas à mourir de faim comme le croyaient les théoriciens de l'Économie, mais presque toujours à un certain nomadisme. (Cf Marshal Sahlins *Age de pierre, âge d'abondance*). Or, le nomadisme, avant la domestication des animaux, repose sur les épaules des hommes et probablement plus encore sur les hanches des femmes, ce qui limite drastiquement au strict minimum le nombre d'objets techniques que l'on peut emporter avec soi. De sorte que le développement technique, aussi sophistiqué et subtil qu'il ait été à l'époque, était ainsi également quantitativement limité.

Le monde dans lequel nous vivons depuis le Néolithique est très différent. La domestication des animaux et la mise en place de l'agriculture ont permis des formes de nomadisme beaucoup plus confortables dans la plupart des cas, et une véritable sédentarisation dans à peu près tous les autres, circonstances qui ont favorisé l'accumulation, non seulement de nourriture dans les greniers ou sur les chevaux et les dos de chameaux, mais aussi l'accumulation de toutes sortes d'objets techniques issus de l'art, de l'artisanat et du commerce.

Ainsi, même si les plantes, les animaux et les lieux singuliers continuaient de hanter l'esprit des hommes, ils le faisaient de manières très différentes... Alors que les chasseurs chez les peuples chasseurs-cueilleurs avaient parfois l'habitude de s'excuser auprès des esprits de leurs proies avant ou après les avoir tuées, les peuples néolithiques se comportaient de manière très différente vis-à-vis de leur bétail. Car le bétail c'est *l'animal-outil*. Et les outils... on les fabrique, on les prend, on les donne, on les oublie ou on les jette quand on considère qu'ils ne sont plus utilisables, ou qu'ils vous encombrent. Les outils, on a le droit d'en user et d'en abuser comme le disaient les lois romaines sur la propriété. Il en va donc de même du bétail aussi, mais avec un peu de modération toutefois, puisque c'est ce que nous mangeons.

Avec le Néolithique, les objets techniques, *animaux et végétaux compris*, sont là quand on les veut et ne sont plus là quand on n'en veut plus. *Le monde est devenu déterministe...* Tandis que dans une économie de chasse et de cueillette, les outils sont toujours trop encombrants, les animaux font ce qu'ils veulent, et les plantes ne font de belles cueillettes que quand elles veulent aussi.

L'esclave, ne peut apparaître que lorsque la population augmente, lorsque les distances intergroupes se réduisent et que les étrangers aux alentours deviennent inévitables, et par suite, les guerres aussi. L'esclave c'est *l'homme-outil* ou plutôt, plus fréquemment la femme-outil. L'esclave en tant que tel n'est pas incompatible avec l'économie de chasse-cueillette, mais il faut le (ou la) nourrir et l'écologie impose à nouveau ses limites à la taille des groupes. Un esclave n'est peut-être pas inapte à la cueillette, mais il est un peu plus épineux de l'envoyer, armé, dans une forêt chasser pour vous. Et si, nomades, vous n'êtes nullement désireux de vous encombrer d'esclaves qu'il vous faudra surveiller sans cesse dans tous vos mouvements, alors vous songerez peut-être à mangez vos esclaves. Mais une fois que vous l'avez fait, il n'y a plus d'esclaves.

Si bien qu'avec le Néolithique, l'univers tout entier ou presque, les plantes, les animaux, la terre et les hommes se sont trouvés transformés en objets techniques. De sorte que les âmes, c'est-à-dire les esprits indépendants qui étaient censés animer les choses sauvages correspondantes, ont disparu, petit à petit, – des cerveaux humains du moins.

Tout ce qui n'était que peu ou pas du tout manipulable dans le monde des chasseurs-cueilleurs est devenu quotidiennement manipulable dans le monde néolithique. Bien sûr, nous avons continué à respecter l'esprit de certains animaux, et jusqu'à aujourd'hui, on trouve des lions, des tigres, des taureaux, des faucons et des aigles, des chênes et des oliviers, sur nos emblèmes, nos devises, dans des logos, sur nos voitures, et bien sûr, sur nos drapeaux. Mais ce n'est plus qu'allégorique. Le cœur et la passion sont partis, et la magie s'en est allée aussi.

Cependant, s'il peut encore parfois arriver à un homme de marcher nu, on peut être sûr en revanche qu'aucun homme n'a jamais marché l'esprit vide. De sorte que les esprits des animaux, des plantes et plus généralement de la nature ayant déserté l'esprit des hommes, il a bien fallu qu'il se remplisse d'autres choses.

Qu'y a-t-il dans la tête d'un homme ?

Eh! Bien... Non. Cette image n'est pas une *vue de l'esprit*. Mais en supposant que l'inconscient soit structuré comme un langage, peut-être que questionner le langage nous ouvrira des portes vers l'inconscient - du moins collectif.

Une analyse cavalière d'un thésaurus d'environ 350 mots et expressions désignant le sexe masculin dans la langue française donne les résultats suivants :

• 46% de termes et expressions liés aux objets techniques ou à la technologie (y compris la technologie de guerre)

• 14% de termes et expressions liés aux animaux ou aux plantes (ex : anaconda, anguille, asperge...)

• 9% de termes et expressions liés à des noms ou prénoms de personnages (ex : Adam, Adolf, Jack, Freddy...)

• 4% de termes culinaires (ex : nem, nouille, andouille, ...)

• 4% d'adjectifs utilisés comme noms (par exemple énorme, inexorable, indomptable, douloureux, ...)

• 3% de diminutifs (ex. zizi, zigounette, zezette, ...)

L'ensemble des termes ainsi analysés représente environ 80 % du thésaurus considéré.

Même en tenant compte d'éventuelles erreurs de classification ou d'interprétations erronées, il faut admettre que l'inconscient collectif lié au sexe masculin semble assez fortement marqué par la technologie et que, si les êtres humains paraissent quelque peu obsédés par le sexe, il apparaît que le sexe masculin lui-même semble quelque peu obsédé par des outils et le travail...

Qu'en est-il des termes et expressions utilisées pour désigner le sexe féminin ?

L'analyse d'un thésaurus d'environ 270 mots et expressions désignant le sexe féminin en français donne des résultats un peu différents :

• 28 % de vocables issus du monde technique - y compris religieux. (par exemple bague, portes, bijoux, autel, mortier, ...)

• 22% de mots liés aux animaux ou aux plantes (ex : brocoli, castor, chat, écrevisse, éléphant, ...)

• 11% de diminutifs (ex : choupette, chounette, conelet, conillon, frifri, mimi, minette, monette, poupoune, foufoune...)

• 6% de termes et expressions géographiques ou géologiques (par exemple caverne, montagne, ruisseau, ...)

• 2% de terminologie culinaire (ex : escalope, pâte feuilletée, pot de miel, tarte aux cheveux, ...)

• 1% de qualificatifs utilisés comme noms (par exemple, baveux, barbu, ...)

L'ensemble des termes ainsi analysés recouvre environ 70 % du thésaurus considéré.

A nouveau la fréquence de la terminologie technique – à condition bien sûr de prendre soin de l'étendre au domaine des objets techniques de la maison, de l'architecture ou du contexte religieux – n'est pas négligeable, quoique moins frappante que dans le cas du sexe masculin. Il correspond à peu près au pourcentage d'occurrences de termes associés aux plantes et aux animaux additionné aux pourcentages d'occurrences de termes issus de la géographie ou de la géologie.

Bien entendu, les thésaurus envisagés, choisis au hasard sur Internet, sont arbitraires, comme peut l'être dans certains cas le choix des classements opérés. Cependant, il serait probablement difficile de trouver des quantités équivalentes de termes techniques désignant le sexe chez les peuples chasseurs-cueilleurs tels que certains pygmées, certains aborigènes d'Australie ou certains « bushmen » d'Afrique du Sud.

Pourtant n'est-il pas surprenant de trouver autant de termes techniques « civilisés » dans un contexte que la religion a si souvent décrit comme le lieu même de l'animalité ?

Ce que le vocabulaire suggère, l'imagerie sadomasochiste le confirme. On peut presque identifier le sadomosochisme à coup sûr à la présence des objets qui se glissent entre les corps : cordes, fouets, costumes, cabinets de tortures, repas érotiques, décors aux allures d'ateliers, automobiles, fantasmes d'esclavage, postures complexes et quasi architecturales, comme chez Sade, etc. Plus encore qu'avec les expressions de douleur si extérieurement semblables à celles du plaisir, dans le sado-masochisme nous sommes dans un Atelier. Dans un atelier et parfois presque dans une usine, comme chez Sade, par exemple, où l'excitation associée au nombre pur atteint parfois une sorte de passion.

Le théâtre sadomasochiste, bien que régi en sous-main par les règles du contrat, aime à être pris au sérieux et veut l'être. Celui des hommes, surtout. Et à cet égard, les boutiques érotiques pour hommes sont très différentes de celles fréquentées par les jeunes femmes puisque de telles boutiques existent désormais pour faire flotter leurs rêveries.

Dans les boutiques pour hommes, on a vraiment l'impression d'être dans un magasin d'accessoires de théâtre où chaque objet s'efforcerait de paraître réaliste. Un objectif qu'il n'atteint habituellement pas, et qui annihile un peu la sombre empreinte de sérieux dont il voudrait s'orner. De sorte qu'il faut généralement se donner un peu de mal pour "y croire".

C'est le contraire dans les boutiques pour femmes, dont l'ambiance ludique du rose scintillant et des strass leur donne un air de joie et où les objets et ustensiles visent indéniablement plus l'élégance des courbes et l'aérodynamisme que le réalisme. C'est un autre jeu, tout différent, le manque de sérieux est total et d'un certain point de vue, du point de vue masculin, presque... inconvenant. Les filles sont probablement plus joueuses que nous, ce qui peut parfois nous sembler légèrement déprimant.

Toujours est-il que l'un comme l'autre lieu ont des couleurs techniques, et que le désir, qu'il soit tissé d'obscur ou bien solaire, est traversé d'objets.

Jeux d'enfants

Il m'arrive parfois, de me souvenir de nos jeux, dans la cour de récréation, lorsque j'avais quatre ou cinq ans. Je me souviens particulièrement de deux d'entre eux. Nous creusions des trous dans le lit de gravier qui recouvrait le sol de la cour, nous nous accroupissions dessus et, très convaincus et pénétrés du sérieux de nos actes, nous couvions des œufs imaginaires. Je suppose que certains d'entre nous avaient inventé ce jeu en observant les poules des fermes environnantes.

Mais nous avions aussi d'autres jeux, aux couleurs plus techniques, qui consistaient à courir les bras écartés dans la cour de récréation en vrombissant à qui mieux mieux. Nous imitions les avions de la base américaine voisine, dont nous incarnions les différents modèles que nous pouvions voir passer au-dessus de nos têtes. Ceux qui nous impressionnaient le plus étaient les « deux queues », appareils à double fuselage qui nous paraissaient très étranges et pour lesquels nous avions une qualité de dévotion particulière.

Je n'ai plus trop l'habitude de visiter les cours de récréation, mais j'ai entendu dire il y a quelques années que les jeux avaient y changé. Maintenant, les gosses se "programment" les uns les autres. L'un s'installe derrière le dos de son camarade et tape sur son pardessus – momentanément transformé en clavier imaginaire – des instructions que l'autre s'empresse d'exécuter une fois la dernière touche « entrée » enclenchée.

Depuis que ces souvenirs me sont revenus, avec les mots et les gestes, je ne peux m'empêcher de penser que les adultes dans leurs jeux sadomasochistes ressemblent beaucoup à ces enfants qui jouent à devenir des choses ou à manipuler d'autres enfants qui ont temporairement décidé de devenir des choses. Cela m'a amené à considérer les aspects « dramatiques » du théâtre sadomasochiste sous un angle différent de celui sous lequel il reste encore souvent perçu. Je veux dire que je le regarde d'un œil amusé, souvent teinté d'humour, mais finalement assez tendre.

Il est difficile d'imaginer à quelle époque ces jeux de masques auxquels nous jouons avec nos choses ont été introduits. Ils sont probablement au moins aussi vieux que l'existence des masques elle-même. Mais il me semble qu'ils révèlent la duplicité de nos choses, qui sont de nous, et qui sont en quelque sorte nous-mêmes, quoique sans être nous et avec lesquelles nous nous sommes longtemps faits enterrer, parfois avec nos femmes, nos chevaux et nos esclaves. Si nos choses ne nous habitaient pas si profondément, si elles n'avaient pas atteint un tel degré d'existence dans les profondeurs de notre esprit, pourquoi tenterions-nous de les emmener avec nous dans les mondes à venir ? Et plus près de nous, qu'est-ce qu'un héritage hors ce ballet des choses où frères et sœurs se déchirent parfois pour une babiole ?

Je me souviens aussi d'un épisode, alors que j'étais encore adolescent et que je bêchais dans le jardin. J'étais assez fier de moi, l'âme sportive et presque stakhanoviste, car j'avais bêché un bout de terrain assez grand, et confusément, plus ou moins consciemment, je me sentais presque aussi puissant et radical qu'une pelleteuse. Et puis ma mère est arrivée, avec un état d'esprit tout différent, et elle a brisé mon courageux élan. "Tu sais," dit-elle, "il faut arracher et enlever les racines, sinon ce que tu fais est inutile car les mauvaises herbes vont repousser".

Ah! Non ! Il avait été assez excitant d'incarner un instant une belle machine, et voilà que ma mère venait me rappeler à la condition ennuyeuse et vaguement indigne d'être humain... Sans compter qu'en plus il fallait se plier en deux, s'agenouiller même parfois, afin d'arracher ces maudites racines. Je me suis arrêté d'un coup et j'ai mis la bêche de côté. Mais ma mère avait tort. Elle venait d'un monde définitivement démodé et hors jeu. Je n'ai jamais vu personne se soucier d'enlever les racines des mauvaises herbes lorsque des gens utilisent un motoculteur.

Pourtant, je vois encore très bien mon père, instituteur à la retraite, fils de paysans pas bien riches, et qui avait alors 80 ans, m'enlevant presque le motoculteur des mains, et traçant des sillons d'un air des plus convaincus, et qui surtout soignait avec amours ses "tournailles", c'est à dire le bout de terrain qu'on ne peut labourer qu'à la fin, car c'est l'endroit qui doit être réservé pour pouvoir tourner la charrue afin de commencer à labourer le prochain sillon dans l'autre sens. Je ne pense pas que le bruit et la puissance assez relative du moteur l'émouvaient beaucoup, mais je pense que cela aurait été un grand plaisir pour lui de mettre un cheval devant le motoculteur. Il n'incarnait pas le moteur mais le labour. Et peut-être dans ces moments là, était-il parfois devenu pour un instant la charrue elle-même! Autre technologie, autres rêveries...

On n'imagine pas toujours à quel point l'âme des choses peut se nicher en nous... Il y a quelques temps, dans les cours de mathématiques, beaucoup d'enfants ne voulaient pas que les lignes droites se coupent. Ils possédaient tous un canif à l'époque et ce qui se passe habituellement en pareil cas leur était bien sûr arrivé : blessures, sang, odeur d'éther, picotements d'alcool, compresses, sparadrap et tout le tralala. Bref, une sorte de désastre effrayant pour un enfant. Et ce sont ces souvenirs qui rendaient les lignes droites abstraites, agressives, dangereuses lorsqu'elles se *coupaient* et bref, insupportables pour eux. Depuis ces temps obscurs et reculés, le monde a changé. Dans les cours de maths les lignes droites ne se coupent plus mais se rejoignent doucement, elles se rencontrent. Ca va un peu mieux. Même si les cours de mathématiques sont restés à peu près ce qu'ils étaient déjà en ces temps obscurs et reculés : un désastre.

Néanmoins, je n'utilise pas personnellement le mot "section" sans une vague appréhension et, aussi raisonnable que je sois, j'écarte ce mot négligemment d'un mouvement d'esprit rapide.

Quant au mot « vivisection », il n'est pas pour rien dans les causes profondes pour lesquelles je ne suis pas devenu médecin mais informaticien. Le silicium ne saigne pas, surtout quand on n'a pas vraiment besoin de trop y toucher.

Il nous faut à tout instant incarner nos outils, nos choses, les imiter, modéliser nos relations avec eux, les laisser nous hanter, dans une certaine mesure, afin d'anticiper les conséquences de leur utilisation et d'éviter les accidents, tout comme nous le faisons d'ailleurs avec les animaux et d'autres êtres humains. Cela ne se passe pas toujours en douceur, ni sans difficultés, ni parfois sans traumatismes.

Feedbacks

Mais cela ne va pas non plus sans effets en retour. C'est à dire que l'ombre, l'esprit, de nos outils et de nos choses nous hante, consciemment certes, comme nous le pensons le plus souvent lorsque nous nous en apercevons, mais surtout inconsciemment, bien qu'on oublie curieusement d'y songer. L'utilisation de nos outils et de nos choses nous change, transforme notre cerveau et bien sûr nos relations avec le monde humain et plus généralement avec le monde non technique.

D'une part, il nous faut dans une certaine mesure considérer nos outils et nos choses comme des alter ego, puisque nous devons les imiter, les mimétiser. Mais d'autre part notre vision à court terme, notre *réalisme*, nous poussent à ne pas accepter cette situation. Notre réalisme ordinaire nous dit de les réduire à ce que nous croyons qu'ils sont, à ce qu'ils sont censés être, de simples êtres fonctionnels, familiers et donc dominés (puisque « domus » signifie la maison familiale). Le Réalisme tient tout entier à cette formule : *"ceci* n'est ***que cela"***.

Nous avons donc tendance à nous en tenir à cette évidence visuelle qu'un outil ou une chose ne sont *que* cet objet qui se dresse devant nous, ce qui correspond d'ailleurs à l'étymologie du mot "object", qui vient du latin *objectum* . *"ce qui est placé avant ou devant*". L'évidence de cet objet, ainsi *jeté devant nos yeux*, nous fait perdre presque immédiatement toute conscience que cette chose a ses racines au plus profond de nous-mêmes. Si profond que nous ne réalisons même pas qu'aucune de nos choses n'a de sens sans ces racines qu'elle plonge en nous. Et ces racines n'incluent pas seulement les "modes d'emploi" de la chose, mais elles intègrent aussi toute la dynamique associée à l'utilisation de cette chose, ainsi que le mimétisme associé à cette chose, que nous devrons interpréter en nous-mêmes si nous voulons l'utiliser correctement et efficacement.

De manière similaire, nous ne nous rendons pas compte que cette chose a aussi des racines dans le monde qui lui est extérieur et qu'elle se trouve en réalité entrelacée au sein d'un vaste réseau de processus qui comprend sa production, l'environnement et le contexte techniques requis pour l'utiliser, ainsi que que les méthodes et précautions requises pour la stocker, pour s'en débarrasser, ou bien pour la réutiliser ou la recycler.

Aussi est-il plutôt affligeant d'entendre tant de gens – y compris bien des gens qui devraient en savoir plus sur la nature du réalisme – dire que leurs outils (téléphone portable, ordinateur, etc.) ne sont « que » des outils . Ils ont acheté un réfrigérateur et ils pensaient qu'il s'agissait juste un outil pour refroidir leur nourriture. Ils ne se sont pas rendu compte que c'était aussi un moyen de détruire la couche d'ozone terrestre. Ils ont acheté une voiture pour voyager plus vite et plus facilement, et ils pensaient qu'une voiture n'était qu'une voiture, sans se rendre compte que c'était aussi un moyen d'envoyer du dioxyde de carbone dans l'atmosphère et de créer un effet de serre.

En fait, aucun objet ne peut jamais être réduit à une fonction, car il fait irrévocablement partie de l'Histoire Universelle et à ce titre il est et reste ouvert à tous les aléas. En dehors du monde humain, rien dans l'Univers n'a de fonction. Et à l'intérieur même du monde humain, la notion de fonction reste indéterminée à tout moment, car elle est constamment subvertie par l'usage imprévu qui peut être fait de tout objet.

Lors d'une de ses conférences, le biologiste théoricien Stuart Kauffman demande au public de lister toutes les usages possibles d'un tournevis. Les mains se lèvent, les propositions fusent de toutes parts et la liste des usages possibles du tournevis ne cesse de s'allonger.

Il propose ensuite au public de lister toutes les utilisations possibles d'un tournevis, mais cette fois, il s'agit d'un tournevis isolé flottant dans l'espace intersidéral, même en prenant en compte qu'un bras humain a pu être ajouté au tournevis pour l'actionner. Et soudain dans la salle de conférence, le public reste silencieux.

Cela prouve que la fonction ne réside pas dans l'objet lui-même, mais dans notre esprit. Dans notre esprit certes, mais pas seulement, car la fonction est aussi dans le contexte. A vrai dire, *toute fonction n'est jamais qu'une rencontre,* quelque chose de l'ordre de l'occasion qui fait le larron. Et si l'on veut bien y regarder de plus près, il apparaît qu'elle ne perd jamais ce caractère quelque peu évanescent, occasionnel, de la rencontre.

La totalité des problèmes écologiques est en fait liée à la phrase réaliste et réductionniste selon laquelle « ceci n'est *que* cela », qui réduit toute chose à ce que nous croyons en connaître. Il devrait mieux se savoir que le réalisme n'est rien d'autre qu'une souricière. Comme Nietzsche l'a souligné en appliquant brusquement le refrain ordinaire du réductionnisme réaliste à l'envers :

> « Le peintre réaliste prétend peindre le réel, mais il n'en peint jamais que ce qu'il sait en peindre. »

Non, "ceci" n'est jamais *seulement* "cela". L'univers est irrémédiablement une aventure à vivre. Ou plutôt, pour mieux dire, l'Univers est une aventure vivante. Ce n'est pas un endroit où il est permis de prétendre s'éviter un peu d'effort en laissant les outils et les choses *vivre* à notre place.

Les problèmes écologiques et sociaux qui résultent de l'aveuglement que porte en elle l'attitude réaliste, montrent qu'il s'agit d'un point de vue faux et dangereux. Nous devrions accepter que nos outils et nos choses ont irrémédiablement un certain degré d'autonomie. Qu'une part de la vie qu'ils mènent – pour ainsi dire – nous échappe. Nous devrions les considérer selon un angle de vue presque animiste (puisque de toutes façons notre inconscient technique les anime et qu'à cela, nous ne pouvons pas échapper). Nous devrions leur témoigner une sorte de *respect techniquement instruit* comme suggéré par Gilbert Simondon... Ce serait probablement une attitude bien plus sage et plus saine que de les considérer plus ou moins comme des esclaves.

À proprement parler, un problème écologique n'est pas un problème de technologie. C'est ce que le vendeur ne nous a pas dit quant à ce qu'il nous a vendu, c'est ce qu'il a « oublié » de nous dire (« par une étourderie de système » comme disait Fourier). Réduire un objet technique à son usage identifié et répertorié, à ce qu'il est censé faire, à ce qu'on prétend qu'il fait, c'est toujours prendre le point de vue de celui qui fait métier de nous le vendre. D'ailleurs, un vendeur ne nous vend pas une chose ou un outil. Il ne nous vend que la *propriété* de cette chose ou de cet outil, mais nullement *l'utilisation* de celui-ci. Que nous l'utilisions ou non n'est pas son problème. Il ne s'en soucie pas. Il vous vend une voiture mais il ne vous vend pas le permis de conduire, ni les cours de conduite assez onéreux qui vont avec. Il ne vous vend pas les pannes ni les accidents de de la route, alors qu'ils font en réalité partie intégrante de la voiture. Il ne vous dit pas qu'en fait ce n'est pas vous qui conduisez votre voiture, mais que que c'est la voiture vous conduit d'une station-service à la prochaine station-service. Et il ne vous dit rien non plus des guerres liées à l'accès au pétrole dans lesquelles vous-même ou vos enfants et vos amis pouvez perdre la vie.

Technologie et Capitalisme

Comme toute type de société humaine, le capitalisme repose sur la technologie mais il n'est en aucun cas identique à la technologie elle-même. Il fait un usage très particulier de la technologie, un usage spécifique, qui exclut en fait l'utilisation finale de la technique, car le capitalisme est basé sur la valeur d'échange et non sur la valeur d'usage.

C'est devenu une attitude très courante et presque une routine de nos jours que de condamner "la technologie", oubliant ainsi que le type de technologie dans lequel nous vivons n'est nullement la technologie "en général", la technologie en tant que telle, mais seulement un sous-ensemble très particulier de technologies telles qu'elles ont été sélectionnées et adaptées aux besoins propres du capitalisme. Cette technophobie résulte à la fois d'une profonde absence d'analyse quant à la manière dont les choses, les outils et les techniques s'articulent à la pensée humaine ou plus précisément au cerveau et au corps humains d'une part, mais aussi et même bien plus profondément de la faiblesse des analyses usuelles de ce qu'est réellement le capitalisme et de ce qu'il fait de la technologie d'autre part.

Presque aucune analyse politique des décisions relatives aux choix technologiques qui se sont trouvées prises au cours de l'histoire du capitalisme n'a été menée. Pourquoi les machines à vapeur nécessitant l'achat de charbon coûteux ont-elles été préférées aux moulins à eau qui n'avaient pas de tels coûts associés ? Pourquoi les voitures individuelles ont-elles été préférées aux tramways et à l'extension des réseaux ferroviaires ? Etc.

Certains savent que Paris a été entièrement reconstruit par Haussman d'une manière qui permettait de faire face beaucoup plus facilement aux émeutes ouvrières. D'autres se souviennent peut-être que l'Internationale Situationniste a clairement indiqué que l'architecture de l'après-guerre, et plus généralement l'urbanisme, avaient été poussés par la nécessité d'imposer l'ordre politique capitaliste et par les exigences d'une répression mentale généralisée. D'ailleurs Dali n'avait-il pas hésité à parler d'une *architecture d'autopunition* ? Mais puisque l'architecture et l'urbanisme sont notoirement des technologies, par quel étrange miracle intellectuel la plupart des gens ne parviennent-ils pas à comprendre que ce qui est arrivé avec l'architecture et l'urbanisme a eu lieu de la même façon pour *toutes* les décisions qui ont été prises quant à *toutes* les technologies utilisées dans le monde capitaliste?

Le fait est que la pensée de la plupart des gens quant à la technologie dépasse rarement le niveau d'autonomie atteint par le végétal. Une plante n'a pas la capacité de se déplacer, elle doit s'adapter à l'endroit où elle pousse, comme si cet endroit était le seul au monde, sous peine de périr. En revanche lorsque le lieu où il se trouve ne lui convient pas, un animal sait qu'il existe d'autres lieux et il s'y déplace. L'absence de pensée technologique conduit les gens à considérer que la technologie actuellement déployée est la seule possible, et ceci pour cette seule raison qu'elle existe. Comme les plantes, la pensée de la plupart de nos contemporains, s'adapte à ce qui est là et elle s'avère incapable de se mouvoir au-delà. Les profondeurs du manque d'imagination humaine sont décidément insondables...

Pourtant, compte tenu des problèmes écologiques en cours et à venir, il devrait paraître raisonnable d'entreprendre un ensemble d'études pour identifier et critiquer les décisions techniques qui ont été prises par le capitalisme tout au long de son histoire. Ceci afin de comprendre pourquoi certaines solutions ont été choisies, quelles étaient les autres solutions possibles, et pourquoi elles ont été rejetées. Cela permettrait de vérifier si les solutions techniques qui ont été rejetées par le capitalisme pourraient être utilisées dans une société non capitaliste ou non. Mais ce type d'histoire politique de la technologie n'est ni entrepris, ni même envisagé et en fait, pas même intellectuellement conçu.

Profondeur de l'empreinte technique

Cette situation révèle un autre aspect de la manière dont la technologie s'est emparée des hommes. Et ceci, qu'ils soient des « geeks », techniquement parlant, ou qu'ils soient tout le contraire d'un « geek », et appartiennent à la foule des technophobes qui non seulement ne se rendent pas compte que leurs vies entières s'appuient sur la technologie mais plus simplempent qu'ils sont littéralement assis dessus. (Oui. Une simple chaise est aussi un objet technique!).

On en est désormais arrivé au point où la technologie hante nos esprits à un degré tel que nous sommes pris dans l'alternative de deux positions opposées qui sont ou bien d'être fans de ce qui est là, ou bien de tout rejeter.

Cela ressemble beaucoup au genre d'opposition binaire, particulièrement stupide et stérile, qui était devenue presque universelle à l'époque de la guerre froide. Il fallait être soit un adepte du capitalisme, soit un adepte du « communisme », sans échappatoire acceptable. Cette époque est passée, mais si les gens ont enfin reconnu le caractère factice d'une telle opposition binaire, cela ne les a pas empêchés de sauter joyeusement dans la suivante.

Un autre aspect de la manière dont la technologie a pris possession des hommes, c'est que l'on entend régulièrement les gens se plaindre de l'énorme gâchis et de l'immense quantité d'ordures et de déchets qui se sont accumulés partout autour d'eux. Ils ne semblent cependant pas réaliser que ce gâchis et ces ordures n'ont qu'une seule origine, qui est le cerveau humain – y compris le leur.

Pourtant, le fait est que le cerveau humain contient forcément le même genre de gâchis, de désordre et d'ordures que le milieu extérieur au cerveau. Et même bien pire, car le monstrueux dépotoir mental qui, via nos cerveaux, commande désormais nos comportements inclut non seulement ce qui a été effectivement produit, mais aussi ce qui aurait pu être produit, ce qui n'a pas pu être produit, ainsi que tout ce dont on a rêvé, et que tout ce qu'on a rêvé de vendre.

Un autre aspect encore de la situation a été mis en valeur par Günther Anders dans *L'obsolescence de l'homme*, avec le concept de *honte prométhéenne*. Il s'agit du sentiment qui envahit l'être humain – notamment ouvrier – lorsqu'il prend conscience qu'une machine peut réaliser bien mieux que lui, plus rapidement et surtout bien plus économiquement, le travail même qui avait fini par faire un peu sa fierté parce qu'on lui avait dit qu'il justifiait son salaire. Se retrouver soudain placé en équivalence avec une chose, c'est à dire *se retrouver* soudain *chose* est évidemment traumatisant, et le fait d'être en même temps licencié n'aide certes pas à surmonter la crise.

Mais l'intoxication des esprits humains par la technique atteint des sommets avec certaines catégories de suicides. Un très grand nombre de gens sont hantés par les outils à un tel degré de profondeur qu'ils se perdent complètement, et en viennent à se trouver accablés par un sentiment d'absurdité globale s'il leur arrive soudain de rendre compte qu'ils sont inutiles.

Ils n'ont pas compris, et ils sont même radicalement incapables de concevoir que les seules choses qui aient une utilité dans l'univers, ce sont les outils, les machines, les objets... Ces gens sont si profondément hantés par les choses, par les outils, qu'ils en viennent à les envier. Ils veulent être utiles, ils veulent avoir un sens, ils veulent *servir*. Servir une cause, servir d'autres personnes, servir quelque chose, quelle que soit cette chose. Qu'importe que ce soit Dieu ou Diable, mais *servir*.

Et leurs esprits s'effondrent soudain lorsqu'ils réalisent que ni eux-mêmes ni l'univers n'ont jamais été destinés à servir à quoi que ce soit ni à personne. Leurs fondations intellectuelles se dérobent encore plus radicalement lorsqu'ils s'avisent brutalement que ni eux-mêmes ni l'univers n'ont jamais été censés *signifier* quoi que ce soit, n'ont jamais été destinés à avoir un sens. Avoir un but, un sens, un usage, une cible, un objectif, est un concept qui n'a de sens qu'à l'intérieur du monde humain, dans le contexte technologique humain. Mais hors du monde humain, de tels concepts n'ont pas de sens. Les gens réalisent soudain tout cela, et sont pris de panique devant ce qu'ils appellent *l'Absurde* et certains d'entre eux meurent de cette découverte effrayante *qu'ils ne sont pas des choses.*

Au delà des sottises, sur l'Absurde qui firent un temps les choux gras des philosophes existentialistes, il faut se représenter que les cerveaux humains se situent juste à la limite, juste à l'interface, entre un univers inutile, une nature vivante inutile, et la bulle technique humaine au sein de laquelle tout a un sens, un propos, un but. Les êtres humains sont indissolublement naturels et culturels. Nier notre appartenance conjointe à ces deux mondes conduit à cette forme de folie rampante et sous-jacente que tout dans l'univers sert à quelque chose. Ce serait là bien rapetisser le monde que de ne lui accorder d'existence que par rapport à un but. Ce serait là le réduire en somme à une création, à la production d'une entité « supérieure » – comme si Dieu pouvait être supérieur ou inférieur à quoi que ce soit, comme si ses actes pouvaient être réduits au résultat de quelque intention *particulière* que ce soit...

C'est au contraire la grandeur, l'immense liberté et le merveilleux caractère de la condition humaine d'être inutile, de n'avoir aucun sens, de ne servir à rien. De se tenir fièrement – et de rester – bien au-delà de tout utilitarisme. Et de se battre quotidiennement pour cela même.

Vivre avec les images

Or, de même qu'il est impossible au cerveau humain de ne pas être hanté par des images – fût-ce même l'image d'un vide pur et total, comme le proposent certaines traditions orientales – il lui est également impossible de ne pas être hanté par les choses, qu'ils s'agisse de choses matérielles et concrètes ou de choses abstraites et « mentales ». C'est ainsi que fonctionnent les cerveaux, et quiconque voudrait se débarrasser de toutes les images, devrait songer à se débarrasser de son cerveau. Décision de quelques conséquences...

Pourtant, s'il n'y a pas moyen de s'évader du monde des images, des outils et des choses, il existe un moyen de *vivre avec* et de parvenir à une sorte de symbiose. Ce moyen, c'est la *Poésie*. Le poète n'est pas moins hanté par les images que les autres, mais la singularité de son approche, c'est qu'*il veut l'être*. C'est là son but, son travail, son art de vivre. Les images sont l'objet même de sa recherche. Mais parce qu'il les accueille et parce qu'il les recherche, en un mot parce qu'il sait *vivre avec*, le poète n'est pas soumis aux images. Il est conscient du jeu que les images jouent dans son esprit. Mais il joue avec les images dans le même mouvement où il est lui-même joué par les images et le sait.

Le processus poétique rend le poète conscient de

l'émergence et du mouvement des images dans l'esprit humain. Là où le non-poète – c'est-à-dire celui qui a oublié qu'il était poète – est manipulé par les images précisément parce qu'il s'y oppose, dénie leur existence et leur jeu, et refuse d'en tenir compte, le poète, au contraire, les laisse entrer en lui, les suit, jusqu'à la transe s'il le faut, mais à la fin il les connaît comme des images et accepte de vivre avec elles. Il accepte la compagnie de cette incessante moire liquide.

Le surréaliste, c'est-à-dire le poète dont l'activité consiste en l'étude et la mise en œuvre collective du fonctionnement réel de la pensée, se trouve dans la position la plus appropriée à se rendre conscient du mouvement des images dans son esprit. Contrairement à ce que les exigences du marché de l'art et de la littérature continuent de faire croire au public, les surréalistes n'ont jamais été ni des hommes de lettres, ni des artistes. On peut au contraire créditer le mouvement surréaliste d'avoir mis un terme aux séparations entre les divers domaines traditionnels d'activités artistiques.

Mais à bien y regarder, il s'agissait en fait d'un retour à cette activité intellectuelle *globale* où la Renaissance s'était brillamment illustrée des siècles auparavant. Nombre des grands artistes de la Renaissance étaient aussi des ingénieurs, des scientifiques et des chercheurs. Piero della Francesca, de nos jours connu essentiellement comme peintre, a été aussi qualifié de plus grand mathématicien de son temps. Brunelleschi était architecte, mais il a également inventé quelques machines, dont un navire à roues à aube pour transporter le marbre. Michel-Ange n'a pas été que peintre, mais fut également architecte. Et tout le monde sait que Vinci n'a pas fait que peindre la Joconde, mais qu'il a également inventé bon nombre de machines, qu'il a été architecte, et qu'il a construit de nombreux automates pour animer les fêtes des princes qui l'employaient.

Ce n'est donc pas par hasard que Marcel Duchamp a mis des moustaches à la Joconde – à la suite d'ailleurs d'un artiste montmartrois qui l'avait représentée fumant une cigarette – mais en manière de clin d'oeil à Léonard de Vinci dont il avait passé quelques années à étudier le travail à la Bibliothèque Sainte Geneviève de Paris. On peut considérer Duchamp, mais il n'est pas le seul dans le surréalisme – ainsi Dali même – comme un héritier de la Renaissance.

Alors que certains surréalistes du passé ont été amenés à ne prendre en considération que l'inconscient freudien, il est très probable qu'il existe une voie possible pour obtenir également un accès à l'inconscient procédural, même s'il s'agit d'un type d'inconscient si habituel et si commun qu'on l'oublie complètement, tout comme l'inconscient freudien d'ailleurs, avant Freud.

Et pourtant, tandis que nous ne nous souvenons pas du moment où nous avons appris à marcher, à parler, et alors qu'à un instant donné de toute conversation, nous ne savons même pas par quelle sorte de miracle nous pouvons réussir à prononcer quoi que ce soit, le langage est devenu pour nous une sorte d'automatisme – même s'il ne s'agit pas vraiment d'un automatisme puisque nous pouvons utiliser le langage pour dire beaucoup de choses différentes et que nous utilisons parfois le langage de manière radicalement créative. Presque tout a été écrit sur le langage et l'inconscient freudien, mais presque rien sur les relations du langage et de l'inconscient procédural qui lui est pourtant sous-jacent et sans lequel nous ne saurions même prononcer un seul mot.

De même, rouler à bicyclette, nager ou même simplement utiliser une fourchette ou une cuillère pour manger, sont aussi devenus depuis longtemps des automatismes. Mais à nouveau, il ne s'agit pas vraiment d'automatismes, puisque nous pouvons adapter et courber ces "automatismes" selon notre volonté, le contexte et les nécessités du moment.

Si l'on admet que le langage est vraiment ce qui fait de nous des êtres humains (ce dont personnellement je doute), si avec Lacan on peut même en venir à considérer que "l'inconscient est structuré comme un langage" (ce qui est très discutable), puisque le langage est un outil, qui se structure différemment selon les langues, alors il doit en aller de même de tout ce qui finit par être aspiré au plus profond de notre inconscient procédural. Il doit donc exister une sorte de sous-bassement commun entre les structures sous-jacentes des langues et celles qui conditionnent et autorisent nos apprentissages techniques.

Ainsi par exemple, on a longtemps pensé et affirmé que le langage humain était caractérisé par "la double articulation". On sait désormais que c'était peut-être un peu rapide et que certains singes sont capables d'articuler différents signaux usuels pour composer des messages adaptés à des contextes sémantiques différents – même s'il ne le font que de manière peut-être un peu rudimentaire à nos yeux.

Mais ce qui devrait attirer l'attention, c'est justement l'usage du terme *articulation* qui, dans cet emploi, est issu du vocabulaire technique. Dès lors, on aperçoit vite que nous avons su articuler nos actes, pour nous déplacer, manger, marcher etc. Bien avant d'apprendre à articuler les mots, les phrases et tout ce que nous articulons de langagier, paragraphes, chapîtres, volumes, bibliothèques, etc. A nouveau, cette capacité d'articulation technique n'est pas spécifiquement humaine. La corneille de Nouvelle Calédonie est capable d'articuler une séquence technique de trois étapes incluant divers outils pour parvenir à ses fins. Je me souviens aussi d'un article sur l'intelligence animale où une photo montrait un chimpanzé monté sur trois caisses qui tentait d'attraper une banane avec un bâton, tandis que l'article voisin s'évertuait à démontrer que les animaux sont incapables de planification...

Les sociétés industrielles démontrent à l'envi que les technologies s'articulent les unes avec les autres (ou se composent) et que *la technique se déploie comme un langage...*

Toutes ces compétences que nous avons acquises un jour et qui sont devenues « automatiques » font partie de nous, et d'une certaine manière, elles *sont* nous. Ou bien devrions-nous restreindre notre vision à ne considérer que ce que nous sommes sans elles ? Ce qui ne peut guère que signifier redevenir comme un nouveau-né. Et nul doute que, ce nouveau-né, nous le restons toute notre vie, et que ce sont ces compétences de base encore non identifiées, ces « pouvoirs perdus », qui ne sont pourtant pas tous perdus, qui nous permettent d'apprendre   et   de   continuer d'apprendre jusqu'à notre mort.

Que pourrions-nous tirer d'une approche poétique généralisée qui, au-delà des mots et du langage serait   étendue   aux   actes   eux-mêmes ? Une nouvelle sorte d'art ? Une nouvelle forme de poésie ? Peut être ou peut être pas. Mais nous ne devrions pas nous en soucier, car le Surréalisme était censé être une aventure et parce que l'art et la poésie n'ont jamais constitué que des *exemples* et non ce à quoi le surréalisme devait être cantonné. "*Nous n'aimons ni l'art ni les artistes*" disait Vaché.

Mais, en étendant le domaine de la poésie aux actes eux-mêmes et aux « automatismes » qui les sous-tendent, nous pourrions étudier comment les êtres   humains   apprennent.   Comment   ils apprennent à la fois « physiquement » et « intellectuellement », transcendant ainsi pour une fois la sempiternelle division corps-esprit. Et nous pourrions étudier quel genre de rôles   y joue la partie inconsciente de nous-mêmes. Quelque chose de similaire à ce qu'a fait Gaston Bachelard à propos de l'évolution historique des conceptions scientifiques, lorsqu'il a créé la notion d'« obstacle épistémologique », et plus tard lorsqu'il a étudié ce qu'il appelait « les imaginations de la matière ». Au lieu de nous lamenter, de la manière la plus laide, paresseuse et passive qui soit, du fait que les machines désormais apprennent, au lieu de nous abreuver d'articles de journaux ignares consacrés au prétendu « deep learning», peut-être pourrions-nous gagner quelque chose en tentant de comprendre comment les êtres humains et les animaux apprennent *vraiment* – et beaucoup plus efficacement que les réseaux de neurones artificiels. Peut-être pourrions-nous nous explorer ces terrains encore largement vierges de l'apprentissage conscient et inconscient, et jouer avec ce que nous pourrions y découvrir. Il ne s'agirait plus alors d'apprendre quelque chose, mais d'apprendre comment pous parvenons à apprendre ce quelque chose.

A un niveau collectif, de la même manière que Vincent Bounoure (Groupe Surréaliste de Paris) et Vratislav Effenberger (Groupe Surréaliste de Prague) et leurs camarades sont passés de l'écriture automatique individuelle à l'écriture automatique collective, puisque nous savons assez que la plus grande partie de l'apprentissage est très probablement basée sur les compétences de l'inconscient (similaires à celles qu'utilise un nouveau-né ou peut-être les mêmes), il serait possible de rechercher ce que pourrait être un apprentissage automatique *collectif.* Ce serait tout à fait conforme à l'extension du surréalisme proposée par Bounoure et Effenberger, dans *La Civilisation Surréaliste (1976)* lorsqu'ils envisageaient d'englober toutes les activités humaines, c'est à dire à la fois celles relevant de l'infrastructure (ie. la production et l'échange) et celles relevant la superstructure (ie. les idées et les représentations), et donc tout le champ de l'expression humaine, comme le terrain de jeu légitime d'une civilisation surréaliste. Non seulement un tel projet s'inscrirait dans la perspective proposée autrefois par Bounoure et Effenberger, mais il nous conduirait aussi plus ou moins directement aux racines inconscientes de toutes les activités humaines, mentales ou non.

Nous pourrions alors nous attendre à récupérer les «pouvoirs perdus» humains comme cela a toujours été un des buts du Surréalisme... Car, après tout, à considérer les choses un peu sérieusement, si les pouvoirs humains perdus ne sont pas présents au cœur des chemins par lequel les nouveau-nés apprennent, sauf à penser qu'ils "tombent du ciel", on voit mal d'où ils pourraient possiblement trouver leur origine. D'ailleurs, tout porte à croire que la manière dont les adultes et les adolescents apprennent, si l'on pouvait l'examiner en profondeur, ne peut pas être si différente de la manière dont apprennent spontanément les bébés.

Car enfin, qu'est-ce qu'apprendre ? C'est construire – en fait, *créer* ! – progressivement une forme abstraite générale et réutilisable à partir d'un magma de perceptions brutes. Une compression de données, mais une compression *prédictive*. Et il faut en effet utiliser ici le terme de « créer », car rien ne prouve que les représentations que construit notre cerveau correspondent à des objets réels. Et la preuve, c'est que nous les modifions et les adaptons sans cesse. Adapter ses représentations, c'est ce qui s'appelle proprement apprendre, et c'est, chez nous, comme chez beaucoup d'autres animaux, une activité de chaque instant.

Cette *création* et cette adaptation des formes, c'est ce dont sont actuellement capables les réseaux de neurones arrtificiels ("formels"). Mais ils n'y parviennent qu'à partir d'un nombre énorme d'exemples – de l'ordre de centaines de milliers à un million d'exemples. Il est bien évident que les réseaux de neurones biologiques de la plupart des animaux – insectes compris – sont autrement plus flexibles et plus « performants ». Et malgré le bruit qu'on en fait, il est assez peu probable qu'un réseau de neurones artificiel actuel s'avère capable d'égaler l'intelligence d'une simple abeille...

Mais si l'on s'en tient à la définition de l'apprentissage proposée ci-dessus, on ne peut s'empêcher de faire le lien avec le problème que posait Matta dans ses *morphologies psychologiques*, c'est à dire tenter de saisir la dynamique de la perception avant qu'elle ne se fossilise en forme. Cependant Matta était un penseur essentiellement visuel et très proche de la problématique de Marcel Duchamp, elle même dérivée de la Relativité et des notions d'espaces à 4 dimensions. Matta abordait les choses selon un point de vue essentiellement géométrique – même si multidimensionnel. Dans ce qui est proposé ici, l'objectif ne serait pas seulement d'étudier et d'atteindre l'aspect visuel du processus d'apprentissage, mais bien *tous* les aspects de l'apprentissage humain, c'est à dire, pour l'exprimer en termes absolument généraux, la façon dont nous entrons en contact avec le monde et la façon dont le monde nous touche et pénètre en nous.

On aurait pu espérer que les successeurs de Matta aux USA, les artistes de l'école artistique qui a été appelée L'Expressionnisme Abstrait s'emparent de la problématique de Matta comme Matta avait repris la problématique de Duchamp. Mais il semble qu'ils aient surtout repris les apparences du Surréalisme, *sa carapace artistique*, plutôt que son esprit. Matta lui-même, reprenant une expression bien connue de Rimbaud, a fini par caractériser ce manque profond d'esprit de l'attitude générale de L'Expressionnisme Abstrait par la remarque suivante : « Le dérèglement raisonné de tous les sens, oui. Mais *pour le sens* ».

Il faut dire aussi qu'à l'époque de la Guerre Froide, où L'Expressionnisme Abstrait s'est historiquement épanoui, l'objectif des gouvernements américains était de favoriser l'émergence d'une forme d'art "occidental" et même plus étroitement "américain" pour faire le pendant de l'art "réaliste soviétique" plutôt "russe". Etrange idée que l'art puisse avoir une nationalité... Mais enfin, la manœuvre a pleinement réussi à tous égards, même s'il n'est pas tout à fait assuré que l'intelligence y ait gagné dans un cas comme dans l'autre.

Il reste que l'extension de la problématique de Matta, qu'on aurait pu attendre par exemple de l'*action painting*, ne s'est pas produite aux Etats

Unis, et qu'elle n'a que partiellement eu lieu en Europe du Nord avec des mouvements comme CoBrA et sous l'influence, par exemple, des idées d'Asger Jorn dont les intutions comme celles de Matta préfigurent la période actuelle.

Au total l'impression générale qui émerge de la période de la Guerre Froide est assez décevante, laissant une sensation d'occasions manquées, d'expérimentations parfois audacieuses mais dont il ne semble pas que beaucoup de leçons aient pu être tirées. Une impression générale qui tendrait à accéditer l'opinion qu'il n'y a pas de progrès en art, ce que la Renaissance, et dans une moindre mesure le Surréalisme lui-même, infirment pourtant de la manière la plus éclatante.

Cependant, la description très cavalière qui a été donnée plus haut de la problématique de Matta apparaît vite incomplète et même injuste dès que l'on considère que l'approche de Matta n'a jamais été réduite à la dynamique du couple perceptions brutes - représentation mais qu'il a toujours cherché à l'étendre aux autres domaines des activités intellectuelles. Il est important de noter que c'est par ce souci permanent que Matta dépasse indiscutablement Duchamp qui, assez étrangement d'ailleurs, ne semble pas s'y être intéressé.

Car contrairement à ce que suggère ce que l'on a désormais appris des réseaux de neurones formels, l'apprentissage ne se résume évidemment pas à une transition entre perceptions brutes et représentation, mais il y a tout lieu de penser que le même type de transitions se poursuit selon des mécanismes peut-être différents ou peut-être similaires dans les divers niveaux d'abstraction du domaine des idées et des dynamiques qu'on peut leur associer (ie. au niveau des modèles).

Quoique ce qui a été développé jusqu'ici n'ait guère concerné que des aspects pour ainsi dire quasi gestuels de l'inconscient, il ne s'agissait en fait que de donner un exemple. Il reste tout autant à élucider la manière dont les idées émergent d'un type d'inconscient qui ne semble pas entretenir de relations très étroites avec la vision freudienne de l'inconscient, quelque peu handicapée par ses origines assez étroitement thérapeutiques. Ce domaine de la dynamique consciente-inconsciente des idées n'a guère été exploré que par des mathématiciens – et non des moindres : Henri Poincaré et Alexandre Grothendieck notamment – souvent attentifs à la manière dont les idées émergeaient en eux-mêmes. La panique assez largement répandue qu'inspire le simple mot de Mathématiques est sans doute responsable du manque d'intérêt aussi étonnant que général qu'ont inspiré les observations des mathématiciens. Que les Mathématiques elles-mêmes puissent inspirer quelques craintes est compréhensible, mais que cela s'étende aussi aux écrits biographiques des mathématiciens eux-mêmes est plus inexplicable.

Eviscération du langage

Cependant, c'est une chose que proposer le projet d'une poésie généralisée, c'en est une autre de parvenir à ce que pareil projet prenne corps... Considérons à titre d'exemple ce qui arrive actuellement au langage et à la poésie dans l'organisation sociale où nous vivons...

L'usage très particulier qui est actuellement fait de la technologie nous éloigne de tout contact réel avec le monde, de *la caresse du monde*. Dans tout ce que nous rencontrons dans notre vie quotidienne, nous sommes *livrés*, au double sens du terme mis en valeur par Gunther Anders dans *L'obsolescence de l'homme*. Nous sommes *livrés*, au sens bien sûr où nous livre les objets « ready made », des objets qui sont de purs *résultats*, c'est à dire privés, dépossédés, *amputés* du procesus de leur genèse. Cependant, par le même mouvement, nous sommes aussi subrepticem*ent livrés*, comme Jeanne d'Arc fut livrée aux anglais, c'est à dire, pieds et poings liés. L'objet est devenu ce que son étymologie suggère : *ce qui est jeté devant* (nous), c'est à dire non plus un éclaireur pour nos aventures, mais *l'obstacle qui nous empêche d'avancer.*

Car nous ne rencontrons plus que des choses ou des outils ou des machines qui ont été préparés en vue d'un *futur déterminé*, c'est à dire pour l'usage auquel ils sont destinés, et qui sont donc prisonniers de cet usage prévu, qu'il soit explicite ou, plus sournoisement, implicite et caché. Mais cet usage prévu ne peut évidemment rien être d'autre qu'une redite, et même une redite de redites. De sorte qu'on retrouve dans l'usage, c'est à dire dans le *futur* de l'objet, le même processus de répétition en série qui l'avait porté à l'existence et qui constituait son passé avant qu'il ne devienne cette étrange *amnésie* qui constitue toute marchandise en tant que telle.

Il est difficile d'imaginer manière plus insidieuse et efficace de diffuser un conformisme avec une exactitude quasi vertigineuse. Les objets font exactement ce qu'ils ont été conçus pour faire et par voie de conséquence, les hommes, lorsqu'ils s'en servent, font *aussi* exactement ce qui a été prévu qu'ils fassent. De sorte que n'est plus du tout le Diable qui se cache dans les détails, mais tout au contraire, c'est un genre particulièrement insidieux et inconscient de *Police*. Si certains informaticiens ont pu dire à propos des logiciels interactifs « *le code, c'est la loi* », ils ne faisaient là que révéler un état de choses bien plus ancien, qui est que chaque objet fait la Police et la Justice, la Loi et les Prophètes. Toute interface homme-machine, homme-outil, homme-objet est conçue pour *déterminer* la manière dont il en sera fait usage. C'est à dire qu'elle détermine jusqu'à nos gestes. Et rien ne prouve qu'elle le fasse avec bienveillance. Mais ni les concepteurs ni les utilisateurs ne semblent s'en soucier. Pour ce qui est des employeurs des concepteurs, on sait qu'ils se soucient surtout de ce que les dites interfaces soient conformes à leurs intérêts financiers. Et c'est là une variété de mèmes dont Richard Dawkins ne semble guère avoir parlé.

Par ailleurs, le principe de la production en série du même, consiste évidemment à exclure tout accident. Notamment cette part d'accident qui s'insinue, qu'on le veuille ou non, dans toute production artisanale. Mais il faut aussi noter toute part d'accident est également exclue de l'usage, qui n'est, dans les pratiques, guère moins répétitif, que ce qui a cours dans la production en série. On masque généralement cette situation quelque peu déprimante en déclarant que l'usage est strictement individuel et qu'il appartient au domaine de la vie privée. Nous vivons ainsi dans un monde hautement individualiste dans lequel tout est produit en série et ou chacun fait donc nécéssairement exactement la même chose que tous les autres, mais prétendument *en secret*. On peut tenter d'y croire, et même étonnamment on y parvient. Ce qui n'empêche pas que rien ne tue l'inspiration amoureuse comme d'entendre le samedi soir le voisin et la voisine se livrer au même genre de pratiques que celle qui vous occupe, à peu près à la même heure et à 30 centimètres de vous de l'autre côté du mur... Ainsi, d'un côté le passé de l'objet est passé à la trappe et de l'autre, le futur de l'objet a disparu dans les profondeurs « mystérieuses » de l'intime. Rien d'étonnant à ce que nous vivions dans un éternel présent, dans cette gloire éternelle de la marchandise qui trône dans sa vitrine.

Cette perte de contact avec le Réel n'est pas seulement individuelle, elle est aussi, et bien plus profondément *collective*. Dans le travail collectif libre, le contact avec le monde réel s'offre aux acteurs d'un processus de production mis en œuvre en commun, qui est créé, exécuté et contrôlé par les acteurs eux-mêmes. Ce processus collectif requiert et *crée* donc nécessairement un langage. Mais lorsque les hommes sont collectivement dépossédés de tout contact avec le monde technique comme avec le monde prétendument non technique de l'usage, quand le travail et la vie hors travail ne nous permettent plus ce contact avec le monde, les capacités poétiques du langage s'amenuisent drastiquement, ou plutôt *s'effondrent*. Et c'est certainement ce que constatait Annie Le Brun dans « *Du trop de réalité* » et encore plus clairement dans « *Appel d'Air* » sans parvenir vraiment à nommer et identifier – pour autant que j'aie pu le percevoir - les causes profondes de cette disparition silencieuse des capacités poétiques du langage courant.

Les mots perdent leur sens et leurs résonances parce que la vie technique quotidienne elle-même perd son sens. Ou plutôt pour la simple raison qu'elle disparaît. Les mots perdent leur sens parce que *le sens est attaché à l'action*, parce que le sens est une révélation, parce que *le sens émerge des incertitudes* dans lesquelles se produit toute action. Tandis que chaque profession avait créé son propre langage, son propre argot – l'argot à proprement parler n'étant que le langage professionnel des voleurs, des meurtriers et des escrocs – lorsque les métiers et les artisanats eux-mêmes disparaissent, et leurs langues particulières avec eux, la langue commune se trouve alors coupée d'une source considérable d'expressions, de mots et même de nouvelles possibilités syntaxiques, pour ne rien dire, même, de l'effondrement sémantique associé.

Les langages des métiers et des artisanats sont intimement pénétrés par l'action. Ils sont toujours lourdement chargées de sens car toute action expose à des risques et requiert donc systématiquement un minimum *d'attention* et de *prudence*. Les métiers et les artisanats intègrent presque toujours des traits dialectaux, traces des domaines où une activité donnée est née, ou bien a atteint son plus haut niveau. Ils font souvent un large usage de métaphores, sexuelles ou non, mais le plus petit thésaurus de ces langues de métiers révélerait facilement leur charge poétique. Tout comme c'est d'ailleurs le cas pour les noms populaires de nombreuses espèces de plantes.

Quand les langues des métiers – c'est à dire les langues du travail humain – se perdent, alors le langage se réduit à cette langue des managers de différents niveaux, dont la fonction essentielle est de *mentir*. Car les managers doivent mentir à leurs supérieurs pour leur faire savoir que tout va pour le mieux mais ils doivent aussi mentir à leurs subordonnés pour les inciter à travailler plus et mieux afin d'augmenter des profits dont ils ne bénéficieront guère ou jamais. Et encore plus souvent, pour les convaincre que la nouvelle organisation du travail, récemment et brillamment conçue par des personnes qui n'ont jamais travaillé, constitue une amélioration notable ou un progrès prometteur.

L'activité des managers consiste essentiellement à ne rien faire, à ne rien créer, à ne rien produire, mais simplement à transmettre des ordres vers les niveaux inférieurs, à destination des producteurs réels, à comptabiliser les résultats et à rendre compte de la bonne exécution des ordres et de l'excellence des résultats vers les niveaux supérieurs. L'art des managers excelle dans le *tableur* (et ses petits dessins extrêmement originaux) ainsi que dans la production de « transparents » aussi élégants que concis, dont leurs supérieurs exigent qu'ils résument la totalité du réel de la pensée en moins de 5 « slides ». Deux « outils » dont la modernité est désormais si fermement établie qu'il y a tout lieu de la croire éternelle.

Il va de soi que le langage lui-même n'a alors d'autre possibilité que de devenir de plus en plus abstrait, de plus en plus « formel » comme le notaient déjà Bounoure et Effenberger dans *La Civilisation Surréaliste* à propos de la vogue du Structuralisme après-guerre. Le langage n'est alors même plus le support du mensonge, mais plus exactement celui du vide, d'un pur néant. Et le type de poésie associé à ce type de langage est l'art très subtil de ne rien dire, tout en laissant croire aux interlocuteurs que quelque chose est dit. En d'autres termes, le mensonge s'est maintenant déployé à l'intérieur même de l'acte de parler. On ne peut évidemment plus du tout parler de langage, il faut parler de simulacre.

Tel est l'état actuel du langage. Et il en est évidemment de même, sinon pire, des images qui visent désormais essentiellement à nous connecter au vide fondamental de l'argent, comme l'illustre *Ce qui n'a pas de prix* le livre récent – quoique peut-être un peu tardif – d'Annie Le Brun.

Or, au revers d'une telle situation, si le champ d'investigation et d'action surréaliste était étendu de manière à englober les pouvoirs inconscients qui permettent aux êtres humains d'apprendre, nous pourrions renouer le contact que notre esprit et notre corps construisent constamment avec le monde lui-même. Un monde que nous ne connaissons en réalité qu'à travers cette activité créatrice permanente de l'esprit et du corps. En d'autres termes, nous renouerions alors avec les sources mêmes de la poésie.

Si l'analyse ci dessus contient un peu de vérité, elle impliquerait donc de nous reconnecter au travail. Je crains que le lecteur ne m'abandonne séance tenante au son de ce simple mot de Travail. Mais non. Il ne s'agit évidemment pas ici du travail salarié, mais de la production collective et libre de la totalité de ce qui constitue des vies humaines. Un art commun de faire, de vivre et de savoir.

Dans la confusion mentale ambiante, on persiste, par une négligence feinte, à appeler un « travail » ce qui n'est en fait presque toujours qu'un emploi. La différence est pourtant fondamentale... Le travail transforme le monde, l'emploi au contraire perpétue l'état des choses existant. Assimiler l'un à l'autre c'est donc dire qu'il n'y a rien d'autre à faire en ce bas monde que de perpétuer ce qui est. On voit l'excellence de la manoeuvre sémantique, d'un effet castrateur sensiblement équivalent au célèbre « There Is No Alternative » de la regrettable Margaret Thatcher. Dans la novlangue ordinaire, « transformer le monde » au sens de Marx devient donc informulable. On ne peut plus qu'être employé au monde,   c'est à dire, par exemple, pour ce qui concerne le journal du même nom, à contribuer à l'interpréter. Quelques lecteurs se souviendront peut-être qu'en des temps désormais immémoriaux,, le mot « Travail » était en Physique un équivalent strict du mot « Energie ». L'énergie – dont il faut rappeler que l'on ne peut ni la créer, ni la détruire, et encore moins l'économiser – constitue en Physique le corrélat inexpugnable de toute *transformation*. L'emploi, lui, ne transforme rien du tout. Il encaisse, enregistre, synthétise, produit des rapports plus ou moins comptables, bref, il gère... L'emploi, finalement, sent toujours un peu le Kafka, c'est à dire l'absurdité bureaucratique, informatisée ou non.

On pressent vaguement que la généralisation de l'emploi conjointe à l'expédition de toutes les formes de travail effectif aux antipodes de la planète ne doit pas être pour rien dans l'immense perte de toute volonté de vivre si caractéristique de l'époque. Tandis que les révolutionnaires des années 1960-1970 pouvaient encore parler de « la volonté de vivre » – malgré déjà l'ombre d'un doute – parler de « volonté de vivre » dans les

« pays développés » au 21ᵉ siècle c'est désormais risquer de déclencher un soupçon d'hilarité – et peut-être même plus qu'un soupçon.

L'anesthésie actuelle est telle que le citoyen des « pays démocratiques » ne saurait plus même être réveillé par l'explosion d'une bombe sur son palier, pas plus que par le canon d'une Kalachnikov pointé sur lui en ouvrant sa porte d'entrée...

Il n'est pas anodin de rappeler que les hommes ne vivent pas seulement de pain, mais aussi, bien plus radicalement encore, de *poésie*. Et *l'ennui* – je pèse ici mes mots – c'est que la poésie a pratiquement disparu, avec le travail, comme je l'ai suggéré plus haut. Et par conséquent le désir de vivre, qui ne tenait que par ce fil ténu de la poésie, a disparu avec elle. C'est à cela que tient cette anesthésie vertigineuse par laquelle se maintient ce qui a tout les dehors d'une addiction irrémédiable au capitalisme. Tout indique que chacun préfère – et de loin – mourir par le Capital que se hasarder à vivre.

La crise écologique en cours démontre désormais qu'à relativement court terme l'alternative est la suivante : ou bien mourir sous la botte des maffias de tous ordres, ou bien se résoudre à produire librement et collectivement la totalité de la vie humaine, ce qui s'appelle travailler, c'est à dire, tout simplement, mettre en place et développer ici et maintenant des coopératives et des réseaux de coopératives.

Le vieux mouvement ouvrier continue de raisonner

comme si le peuple, était encore dépourvu de moyens de produire. Mais ces moyens, le Capital nous les a vendus. Ils sont partout – endormis dans les placards, les caves, les greniers, les garages et les ateliers. Il n'est pas même besoin de modifier les règles de la propriété privée, il suffit de *changer les pratiques*, de les mettre les moyens existants en commun et de s'en servir. Certes, la qualité de ces outils, généralement issus de la regrettable République Populaire de Chine, ne les rend pas exactement durables, mais enfin, c'est assez pour apprendre, pour s'instruire collectivement et progresser.

Voilà. Il me semble avoir exposé ici quelques uns des moyens propres à recouvrer à la fois la liberté et la poésie, d'une manière plus profonde qu'il n'a pu être jusqu'ici suggéré. La crise écologique en cours et l'effondrement probable de la civilisation actuelle vont de toute évidence nous y contraindre. Le jeu est à la fois risqué et subtil et l'absence vertigineuse de toute volonté de vivre rend actuellement le succès assez improbable.

Sans une longue et progressive accoutumance au travail collectif libre, sans la résolution pratique des problèmes associés, on peut être assuré que chaque « Grand Soir » ne fera que reconduire une nouvelle mafia, qu'elle soit d'un type "soviétique", "chinois", "illibéral" , "sicilien" ou autre. Car les problèmes que pose la mise en place de collectivités de travail libres ne sont pas nécessairement simples, et ils ne se résoudront pas par la magie de quelque « Grand Soir » révolutionnaire que ce soit.

A ce point de l'exposé, je dois bien admettre qu'un
tel projet n'a presque aucune chance de rencontrer
la moindre adhésion au sein les cendres tièdes de
ce qui fut un jour l'aventure surréaliste. Le
Surréalisme est aujourd'hui réduit à l'exploitation
artistique, littéraire ou poétique plus ou moins
malheureuse d'une veine qui avait pourtant à
l'origine ouvert un champ de pensée et d'action
d'une portée autrement plus large, et qui s'était
chargé d'ambitions beaucoup plus vastes. Et bien
sûr, j'ai conscience de cette situation, mais je ne
l'accepte pas.

2018-2021

183